ADVANCED TRAINING FOR THE HOME GUARD

ADVANCED TRAINING FOR THE HOME GUARD

WITH TEN SPECIMEN FIELD EXERCISES

BY

JOHN BROPHY

Author of *A Home Guard Handbook*
and *A Home Guard Drill Book*

The Naval & Military Press Ltd

Published by

The Naval & Military Press Ltd
Unit 5 Riverside, Brambleside
Bellbrook Industrial Estate
Uckfield, East Sussex
TN22 1QQ England

Tel: +44 (0)1825 749494

www.naval-military-press.com
www.nmarchive.com

In reprinting in facsimile from the original, any imperfections are inevitably reproduced and the quality may fall short of modern type and cartographic standards.

CONTENTS

CHAPTER	PAGE
AUTHOR'S FOREWORD	9
I. NEW METHODS OF WARFARE	11
II. TACTICAL RESOURCES AND DISPOSITIONS	29
III. SOME SPECIAL PROBLEMS	55
IV. FIELD EXERCISES AND LEADERSHIP	70
V. TEN SPECIMEN FIELD EXERCISES :	
NO. 1. CLEARING A SMALL WOOD OF ENEMY ON FOOT	88
NO. 2. DEFENCE OF A VULNERABLE POINT BY OUTPOSTS	93
NO. 3. ATTACK ON A FARM	99
NO. 4. HOLDING A FORTIFIED STREET AGAINST ENEMY WITH TRANSPORT	105

CONTENTS

		PAGE
NO. 5.	DEFENCE OF A BRIDGE OVER A RIVER OR CANAL	111
NO. 6.	DEFENCE OF A FACTORY	115
NO. 7.	A SMALL ENEMY PARTY IN CHALK PIT IS ATTACKED WITH MACHINE-GUNS AND HAND-GRENADES	121
NO. 8.	ATTACK ON AIR-BORNE TROOPS	126
NO. 9.	THE ENEMY MASKS THE MAIN DEFENCES AND BY-PASSES TO THE WEST	132
NO. 10.	THE PINCERS MOVEMENT AND COUNTER-STROKE	137

AUTHOR'S FOREWORD

THIS Handbook is intended to supplement and not in any way to replace the official Training Regulations and Operational Instructions for the Home Guard, to which in most respects it conforms. It will be found that in general I have wasted little time on those subjects which the Regulations and Instructions deal with in detail, while discussing with practical applications problems about which, for good reasons, only general principles have been laid down.

By and large this third Home Guard Handbook of mine is to be regarded as a personal view (but one based on administrative experience in an active Company) of the task confronting the Home Guard at this stage of its development. I am most grateful to certain officers of the War Office Training Directorate for their unfailing kindness, patience and courtesy in reading my manuscript. While I have, very gladly, incorporated their suggestions and amendments, all views and statements in this book are my sole responsibility.

JOHN BROPHY.

CHAPTER I

NEW METHODS OF WARFARE

THE Home Guard is a large force of volunteer soldiers, to all intents and purposes unpaid, a military force of which each component unit works alone and never sets eyes on more than half a dozen other units. Its operational plan might be described as a nation-wide dispersal of small concentrations. The basic idea is that each locally raised body should remain in its own district, to keep guard and to give battle there against any invaders who appear, no matter whence they come and whether by sea, land or air.

The Home Guard is now an integral part of the British Army, one of the three fighting forces disposed, equipped and trained for the defence of the country. It is differentiated, however, from the rest of the Army by its dispersal into local concentrations, by its specialised function in the event of hostilities on the soil of Great Britain and Northern Ireland, and by the fact that until such hostilities are in immediate prospect its members do their soldiering in their spare time, and continue their normal employments, producing the country's wealth and paying their share of the heavy taxation which is necessary to prosecute the war to a successful conclusion.

It will be seen that the Home Guard is something unique in the history of this country; indeed, of any country. Volunteer forces, trained bands, "fencibles," and local levies have been raised before, but never have there been so many as a million and a half such men under arms providing means of defence for every parish.

Home Guardsmen consist chiefly of men over and under the age for normal military service—the age limit is seventeen to sixty-five—with a substantial minority of men in the prime of life who are not permitted to join the full-time armed forces because they belong to trades and professions essential to the national effort. On a conservative estimate at least fifty per cent. of the Home Guard are soldiers between forty-one and fifty-five who saw service in 1914–18, men who have proved themselves under fire in a long, arduous and ultimately victorious war against the same enemy they are now called on to face once again. The Home Guard thus possesses one of the most inestimable advantages of a first-class army: it blends maturity and experience with youth and dash.

It was called into being in May, 1940, through a broadcast given by Mr. Anthony Eden, and was for a time known as the Local Defence Volunteers. The call was made because the general military

NEW METHODS OF WARFARE

situation had undergone a drastic change for the worse, owing to the swift and devastating Nazi invasion of the Low Countries and France. The German panzer or armoured divisions, using dive-bombers as forward artillery and parachutists or other air-borne troops as cavalry, and aided by organised treachery behind their opponents' lines, cornered the British Expeditionary Force (but could not prevent the vast successful evacuation from Dunkirk), over-ran Holland and Belgium, and put France out of the war—all in the space of a few weeks. The whole coast of Europe from Norway to Normandy was in enemy hands when the first quarter-million of the L.D.V. began to do their nightly guards—and some of the Nazi troops were only twenty-one miles away.

Since then the Home Guard has kept its vigils without ceasing. It has been armed and equipped; it has completed its defence measures; and it has developed and pursued its training in accordance with its aims and the part that it will be called on to play in repelling an invasion. A year of organised training, each unit adapting the instructions from general headquarters to its own particular needs, has not only greatly increased the size and power of the Home Guard, but replaced its sometimes haphazard and amateurish beginnings with a strictly utilitarian and up-to-date proficiency befitting a professional army in the middle of a great war.

But in those twelve months the strategical and tactical development of warfare has not stood still. There have been important campaigns—one in East Africa, two in Libya, and one in Greece—and the last two have thrown much light on what it is reasonable to expect if and when the Nazis attempt to invade Great Britain.

In Abyssinia, Eritrea and Somaliland the warfare has been of a specialised kind; but in Greece and Libya a good deal of valuable information has been gained about the new kind of *blitzkrieg* tactics. Forewarned is forearmed only if the warning is understood in specific as well as in general terms, and things which have happened in the north of Africa and the south-east of Europe are very much to the point for Home Guardsmen whose fighting will be done more or less on their own doorsteps.

The first campaign to be considered is General Wavell's in Libya, which took his men through the eastern province up to Benghazi at breathtaking speed. This provided a lesson as well as an immense stimulus to British morale. It proved first that the Nazi success in France and the Low Countries had been due not so much to the men in the tanks as to the tanks themselves. It proved that British armoured divisions and mechanised infantry could do what their German counterparts had done—and more: for the Italians in Libya had a huge preponderance in numbers and even

NEW METHODS OF WARFARE 15

a considerable superiority—of numbers—in the air. Despite this, most of their army was routed or captured, and the rest driven back at breakneck speed.

In the second campaign, the German General Rommel caught the weakened British forces on the wrong foot, and with a German panzer force in the van drove the British back almost to where they started from. And this despite the fact that the Nazis lacked what they probably consider adequate dive-bomber support. There are, however, two illuminating contrasts which can be made without the undue bias which springs from optimism and partisanship. First, the advancing British did not merely penetrate the coastal defences but put out of action large Italian forces; while, on the other hand, the Germans when they entered Africa captured only a small British force, and had to leave Tobruk intact on the flank, a fortress, supplied from the sea, which took heavy toll of their attacks and raided their lines of communication. And, second, the German mechanised advance, though swift, was brought to a halt in time to allow reinforcements to be concentrated in a defence system covering Alexandria.

Before drawing any conclusions useful to the Home Guard, let us turn to the short campaign in Greece. A force of sixty thousand British and Imperial troops (necessarily weakening the Libya-Egypt defences) was landed for a campaign which had to be undertaken but which was known from the first to be full of hazards and to involve fighting against superior numbers and fire-power. As it turned out, hazards and disadvantage became disaster: the Jugo-Slavs were unable to offer any effective resistance at all, having mobilised too late, and a large part of the Greek Army was enveloped and forced to surrender. In such circumstances it might well have been expected that the British and Imperial forces would meet with the same fate. The withdrawal enforced on them robbed the R.A.F. of adequate landing grounds, and the British infantry had to carry out its fighting retreat against a vast preponderance of tanks and dive-bombers. Yet seventy-five per cent. of the total force was successfully evacuated, and the German assault troops suffered heavy and perhaps disabling casualties. At any rate, they did not press their attack closely and decisively.

These are the essential facts of recent land war since the Nazi's surprise onslaught in the spring and summer of 1940. There are, I believe, at least six deductions of the utmost importance which can legitimately be made from these facts.

1. *An army weaker than its opponents in fire power and penetrative power may escape destruction but cannot hope for decisive victory.*

In applying this conclusion to the Home Guard it is essential to remember that, although units may have to fight for periods more or less in isolation, the Home Guard is not by any means the sole instrument of defence for this country. In one sense it should be regarded as an integral part of the whole Army, with a specialised and essential function of its own, and in another sense as a kind of fourth instrument of defence—after the Navy, the rest of the Army, and the Air Force. Because the Home Guard is organised in small local concentrations and necessarily equipped only with light weapons, it cannot and should not undertake the destruction of any considerable enemy force. In practice this will usually mean that a Home Guard unit acting alone and faced with a more powerful body of the enemy, will avoid close contact except in circumstances of its own choice, and content itself with a harassing function, obstructing and delaying the enemy in every possible way and inflicting the maximum damage and casualties at the least cost to itself. On the other hand, it must lose no opportunity of falling decisively on smaller, weaker enemy bodies, detached or resting or battle worn; very often it will be able to make these opportunities for itself.

In the event of invasion many Home Guard units must face this grim prospect: that so far as their limited knowledge of the moment goes, they will be up against stronger enemy forces. But they will have these consolations: such a situation will last only for a limited time; and, if they

B

adapt their tactics to their own strength as compared with that of the enemy confronting them, they will by harassing operations be contributing immensely to the defeat of the invasion and ultimate victory. The local superiority which the enemy in some places may be able to establish against isolated Home Guard units will last only for a short time because, so far as informed calculations can foresee, the most formidable invading force the Nazis can land must be inferior to the British defence forces as a whole, not only in numbers but in arms, in fire power and penetrative power. In brief, the situation which occurred in France and in Greece will not be repeated here. The boot will be on the other leg, and the Nazis for the first time will be up against greater strength than they possess themselves. The effects of this on their morale are discussed below under conclusions 5 and 6.

2. *Armoured divisions are more formidable if their supporting air force has a local superiority, but even without this aid they can make considerable and swift advances.*

Hitler did not attempt the invasion of Britain in the summer and autumn of 1940 because his Luftwaffe was unable to beat the Royal Air Force over Britain. He lost 2,375 planes between August and October, while R.A.F. losses were less than one-third of this figure. Everything that has

NEW METHODS OF WARFARE 19

happened since indicates that this superiority in quality of men and machines has been maintained, while every day that passes brings the R.A.F. nearer to a numerical superiority. By and large, it follows that, if and when Hitler resolves at last to invade, the R.A.F. will have the whip hand of the Luftwaffe. At certain times and places German dive-bombers may be able to concentrate and blast a way through opposition for the panzer divisions. At many other times and places the R.A.F. will be calling the tune. Nevertheless, although deprived of full air support, the panzers will be able to advance—as General Rommel's counter-attack in Libya proves. Yet while the panzers must always be regarded as formidable, their advances will be difficult, slowed up by each Home Guard unit they encounter, and sooner or later they will be broken up by the counter-weapons of the Regular Army. That will be the time for the Home Guard to change over from harassing tactics to local offensives, to fall on and destroy panzer detachments shattered by the heavier attacks.

Again, while it is true that the panzers can maintain their advance for some time without full air support (as in Libya), even with this air support and every advantage it does not follow that they can knock out a well-armed force inferior in numbers. They failed to do this in Greece. The panzers can be summed up as still formidable, but not so formidable as they appeared in the summer of 1940, and by no means all-conquering or unconquerable. They are decidedly not supermen in super machines.

3. *The British can employ the characteristic blitzkrieg tactics—armoured divisions using planes as artillery and followed by motorised infantry—just as effectively as the Germans.*

The tank is a British invention, and the further development of its use—at increased speed, probing for weak points to penetrate to back areas, and in self-sufficient units equipped with their own artillery, air force, motorised infantry and engineers —was also a British discovery. There is no point at this time in discussing why the discovery was not exploited, why the Germans were allowed first use of the idea. What is important is to note that General Wavell's campaign in Libya proves that the lesson has been learned well, if late. The mechanised strength of the British Army, reinforced not only from home factories but from the U.S.A., is growing fast. During an invasion Home Guardsmen can therefore expect to see more whirlwind attacks going past them from British armoured forces than from German. In these the Home Guard will have little or no direct part to play. But British blitzes will create, and very suddenly, havoc and demoralisation among the invaders, and the Home Guard must be quick to seize on these opportunities. They must be first obstructionists and reporters, and later the moppers-up of the battlefield.

4. *British tanks and anti-tank weapons are more effective than the German*

The fact that the British and Imperial troops, not merely outnumbered and almost surrounded, but out-tanked and out-gunned, were able to withdraw successfully from Greece, after doing far more damage to the enemy than they themselves suffered, proves that the British technical superiority demonstrated in the air also holds good on the ground. Time and the factories will add quantity to quality. But even if invasion occurs to-morrow, the invaders will have to face superior weapons in superior numbers. Moreover, their reinforcements and supplies will be difficult to come by.

In war, nothing is certain and nothing predictable: every eventuality must be examined and so far as possible foreseen. The Germans may have some unpleasant surprises to spring on us, yet even surprises cannot be manufactured overnight. On a general conservative count of resources and probabilities, it seems that the advantage during an invasion must lie with us. Until the enemy concentrations are manifested, the full concentration of striking power to reply to them cannot be mustered exactly where it is needed. Any Home Guard unit may find itself up against a very stiff proposition, but it should always keep in mind these basic facts. Let it do its duty to the full extent of the means and skill at its disposal, and sooner or later (probably sooner) the Regular Army will arrive to transform the situation.

5. *Morale cannot adequately take the place of weapons, but morale is still a decisive element in determining the issue of a battle.*

Morale means, by and large, the confidence which the soldier has in himself, in his leaders and in his comrades. It is not merely unjust but bad generalship to ask men to oppose their flesh and their wills to an overwhelming superiority of weapon-power in the enemy. Nevertheless, in such circumstances, morale has worked wonders, as recently in Greece, and before that in Libya where superior Italian forces, of poor morale, were not merely routed but rounded up.

The Home Guard being a lightly armed, dispersed, and in some respects a guerrilla army, there may be some severe strains on its morale. On such occasions the high percentage of 1914–18 soldiers in its ranks should prove invaluable. It is equally important that most commanders should understand—and act on—the limitations of the Home Guard arms, avoiding if possible a decisive engagement where the enemy has a local superiority, but, on the other hand, seizing every opportunity when the advantage changes. The basic morale of the Home Guard is high, and will remain high. Provided the men are intelligently led, action will improve it. There are no hard and fast rules for achieving and maintaining a high morale, but many of the principles of leadership (on which it largely depends) are discussed with specific references in Chapter IV of this book.

The other point to be borne in mind is the morale of the enemy. Nazi morale, by all indications, is also high. But it is sprung from an intense emotional surrender of individuality to Hitler, and on past successes. Even allowing for the suppression and distortion of news in the German Reich, the elation of success must have been diminished to some extent by the casualties in Greece, by the spectacular defection of Rudolf Hess, and by the continuance of the war together with the further postponement of the invasion of Britain, as well as by the unconcealable effects of R.A.F. bombardments of Germany.

It seems fair to assume, then, that a Nazi invasion force arriving in this country will be in a state of extreme nervous and emotional strain, fervid in its loyalty to its Fuehrer, both relieved and exhilarated that at last Britain is to be attacked with full force, and calling on memories of past successes to help it meet the exigencies of the present and the immediate future. From this tension of the emotions and nerves (backed by considerable martial and technical ability) it will draw the dynamic power to land and to strike at our defences—and these dynamics should not be under-estimated.

But such a mood contains within itself the seeds of its own destruction. Tough as these chosen Nazi troops may be, they are subject to the limitations of human flesh and blood. They can be super-charged only for a short length of time. Once their self-confidence is broken—by insufficient success and the strain and exhaustion of war—the reaction may well be disastrous to them.

And burrowing in their self-confidence all the time, like a worm, will be certain doubts and certain memories. There will be the question if, after all, the war so far has not been too good to be true. There will be the question why the invasion was so long postponed and if, now it has come, it is not more difficult than ever. And there will be the memory, whether it is personal or taken from books and conversation, of the 1914–18 war which Germany seemed to be winning almost to the end only to collapse and surrender. There will be the memory of any amount of Nazi propaganda afterwards proved false. There will be the memory that the British have always proved tough and unconquerable—and why not again?

NEW METHODS OF WARFARE 25

These are the sort of secret thoughts which will be nagging somewhere in each invader's mind even before he lands in a country where he will be a hated stranger, where hostility will spring at him from every side. At first he will keep his misgivings in his subconscious mind, but as he takes harder and harder knocks they will grow louder and more insistent. He will come hoping for swift success. He may get a little of it. But as he sees his comrades killed, his tanks and planes destroyed, as he is harried by day and night, as fresh opposition meets him everywhere, and the final victory—the only victory which can deliver him from his plight—is still postponed, his morale must begin to crack. And that will be the time for the Home Guard to come in and deliver, in all parts of the country, knock-out blows to the scattered invasion forces.

6. *Panzer divisions as used by the enemy are instruments of terror. If they fail to create panic, or if they are steadily obstructed and delayed, a law of diminishing returns operates, and they progressively weaken in their function.*

The success of German mechanised units hitherto has depended on their speed of movement, their ability to disorganise and demoralise the opposing forces, and the panic they have set up among the civilian population. The plan came off in Poland, the Low Countries and France. It could not prevent the evacuation from Dunkirk (partly owing to the German choice of France as the first enemy to be disposed of) or from Greece —where British counter weapons, nearly twelve months later, had improved. Above all, it spent itself rapidly in General Rommel's advance in Libya, which left Tobruk as an intact and offensive fortification in the rear and was halted at the Egyptian frontier.

Unless they gain immediate and large scale success, panzer divisions rapidly lose confidence and effect. Operating in this country, they would not spread panic among the civilian population to anything like the extent that was observed in Poland, Belgium and France. British civilians have stood up well to heavy air bombardments, and while invasion would furnish a still stiffer test, the presence of a Home Guard unit in every parish should provide an immense stiffening of morale. In this way, the first terroristic effects of the panzers—on unarmed men, women and children— should be severely diminished. And here it is well to remember that Nazi tanks will not wish to waste ammunition, which they know perfectly well they may not be able to replenish. They will not dare to stop anywhere for long: their aim will be to go through rather than to scour a district. They will hope to get the greater part of their terroristic effect not from what they do, but from what people

NEW METHODS OF WARFARE 27

expect them to do, and from exaggerated reports of their activities spread by rumour. The Home Guard can do a great deal by precept and example to rob them of this weapon.

Secondly, the terroristic aim of the panzers will be turned against the individual troops opposed to them and the organisation of these troops. They will hope to achieve success largely by creating demoralisation and operational chaos all around them. It is precisely to counteract this aim that the Home Guard is organised in local concentrations, each holding its own territory but highly mobile within that territory. The Home Guard in effect forms a network over the whole country, a network of obstructive but elastic defence systems. Each unit will adapt its tactics to the strength of the force opposing it at any moment, harassing and delaying (and reporting) powerful enemy bodies, destroying smaller ones. Because it is decentralised, the Home Guard will be difficult to disorganise. The national network of the Home Guard defences will catch and cling to and finally help to wipe out all the invading forces. The terror will be met with skill and resource, as well as courage, and when the terror fails the panzers will progressively become easier to overcome.

The training of the Home Guard has passed through two distinct stages. At first, in the summer and autumn of 1940, it was largely improvised, dependent to a considerable extent on the experience of the old soldiers in its ranks, yet chiefly directed towards meeting what then seemed the paramount danger—parachutists. *A Home Guard Handbook* was written at that time and to meet the needs of that situation, and much, if not all, of it is still very much to the point.

Then in the late autumn and winter a period of intensified training set in, with the aim of consolidating the basis of all military efficiency and making Home Guardsmen familiar with several new weapons put into their hands. *A Home Guard Drill Book and Field Service Manual* was written as an aid to this winter training.

By the early summer of 1941 it became apparent that several new developments in warfare had taken place and in particular that the Home Guard must be prepared to play its part in repelling swifter and more heavily armed enemy forces in this country. The emphasis had shifted to take in the tank as well as the parachutist. Also new weapons and new tactics were needed. It is to this end that *Advanced Training and Field Exercises for the Home Guard* has been written. Everything in the chapters which follow should be studied in the light of the new methods of warfare, and the conclusions drawn from them, which are discussed earlier in this chapter.

CHAPTER II

TACTICAL RESOURCES AND DISPOSITIONS

Defence Works.—There are two main kinds: prepared defences which, in the event of action, are to be garrisoned and held in the face of the enemy, and temporary or casual defences which may be made use of in the course of mobile operations.

Prepared defences include road obstacles, usually sited in defiles and of some solidity: pillboxes of concrete, brick or other material: sandbagged breast-works (which may, and in fact should if possible, be more than breast high): weapon pits and fire trenches: roadside bombing pits for anti-tank weapons: reinforced and loopholed walls: reinforced buildings or rooms in buildings.

The first essential is that the prepared defence should afford a good field of fire against the advancing enemy. Wherever the ground permits, alternative positions of equal value should be constructed, and a crawl trench or other protected communication should connect each pair of alternative positions. All should be concealed from air observation. Next, it should provide adequate cover for its garrison against enemy small arms fire.

(See *Field of Fire*, p. 33.) Whenever possible it should give cover also against small shells, mortars, hand grenades, observation from the air and machine-gun fire from the air.

Here are some of the thicknesses necessary to provide protection against small arms fire:

Sandbags filled with sand	40 inches
Sandbags filled with clay, earth or chalk	36 ,,
Brickwork, with lime mortar	14 ,,
Brick rubble between 1-inch boards	12 ,,
Reinforced concrete	12 ,,
Loose chalk	48 ,,
Loose clay	60 ,,
Loose or beaten earth	60 ,,
Timber	48 ,,
Mild Steel Plate	$1\frac{1}{2}$,,

Cover against hand-grenades in breast-works or trenches open at the top is best provided by wire-netting which slopes sharply like an angled roof. It should be so arranged that the grenades will slide off behind a sandbag wall. If this device is adopted two entrances should be arranged to the breast-work or trench where the wire-netting does not impede, and a sandbag wall built inside to take the blast of any grenade entering here.

Cover from air observation is achieved by the siting and camouflaging of the whole defence

TACTICAL RESOURCES AND DISPOSITIONS 31

work. (See *Camouflage*, page 37.) Protection from shells, mortars, air machine-gunning and splinters from air bombs is best effected by providing walls of adequate depth and thickness. Trenches should not be dug, where avoidable, in ploughed fields: the earth is apt to expand and push in the sides.

Weapon pits are short lengths of separate fire trenches. They may be shaped with short transverse arms, like a cross; the advantage is that if a tank or airplane enfilades the trench the garrison can move quickly into the transverse arms (or out of them) where the enfilade fire cannot reach them. The same principle applies to bombing pits at the side of a road from which anti-tank weapons are to be used at close range.

Pill-boxes should not be regarded as exceptionally strong defences. They are very good while the enemy is at fairly long range, but if he is allowed to come close, grenades may be put through the loopholes with disastrous effect. A stout sandbag wall should be built inside all concrete or brick strong-points, against the wall immediately behind each loophole. This will use up some space, but will absorb bullets entering through the loopholes and prevent dangerous ricochets. Plans should be made for the garrison to evacuate every pill-box if the enemy forces his way too near; they should move to an alternative position near at hand, but one of different construction.

Road obstacles should be provided with all-round defence and covered with fire from well-chosen strong points; in addition there should be posts, appropriately armed, *in front* of the obstacles to attack immediately any enemy halted by it. (See *Tank Traps*, page 42.)

Prepared defences should be protected with barbed wire to hold up the enemy seeking to come to close quarters and entangle him where the garrison can bring effective fire to bear. The wire should be concealed in a hedge or other natural feature; it more than doubles the effect if the enemy does not discover it till it holds him up. The wire should be not less than 30 yards—to keep the enemy out of grenade range—and not more than 100 yards in front of the point it protects.

Temporary or casual defences are intended to be used, usually in open country or woods, if mobile operations move that way. They will usually consist of small sandbag walls, about three feet high, or sandbag reinforcements to a ditch or tank. The danger is that they may be occupied and used by the enemy. They should therefore be concealed by bushes or bracken or turf. As a general rule it will suffice if the Home Guard units rely on their local knowledge to find cover, protection and effective firing positions in the event

TACTICAL RESOURCES AND DISPOSITIONS 33

of mobile operations, and erect as few temporary defences as possible. They should, however, reconnoitre each subdivision of their territory to select the best sites, and commanders should make sure that this knowledge is put to good use in field exercises. (See also Chapter IV of *A Home Guard Handbook*.)

The Field of Fire.—By this is meant the length of the ground in front of a firing point which can effectively be brought under fire, and also the width from side to side. As a general rule machine-guns should be able to hit any unprotected enemy showing up to 600 yards in front of them, and to traverse their fire to the same depth through an arc of 180 degrees. For rifles the most effective range is 200 to 300 yards. Ditches, sharp dips in the ground, and houses near at hand invalidate an otherwise good field of fire. The most notable exception to this principle is when a prepared defence commands a street or a road. Here it is only rarely possible (or even desirable) that the weapons should command much more than the width of the road: the idea is that the enemy should be trapped in a defile. Nor is the full range of 600 yards or more essential.

In taking aim at an advancing or halted enemy fire control is important. Only under very exceptional circumstances should the garrison be allowed to select and fire at their own targets.

34 ADVANCED TRAINING FOR HOME GUARD

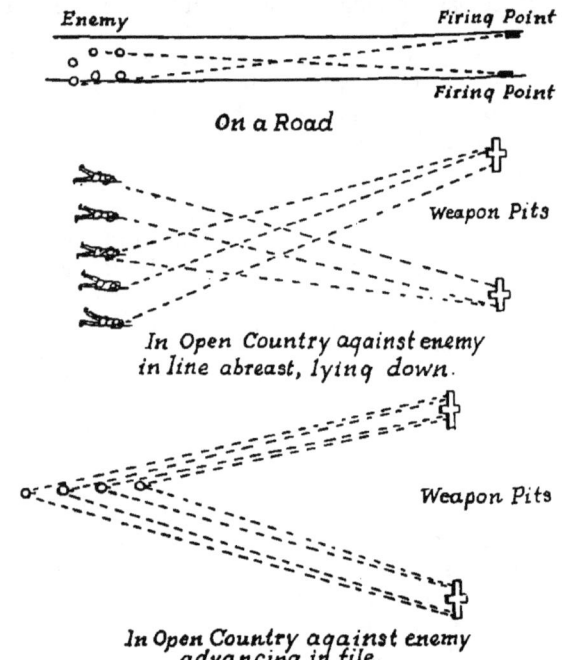

Diagram 1   The Value of Cross-fire

TACTICAL RESOURCES AND DISPOSITIONS 35

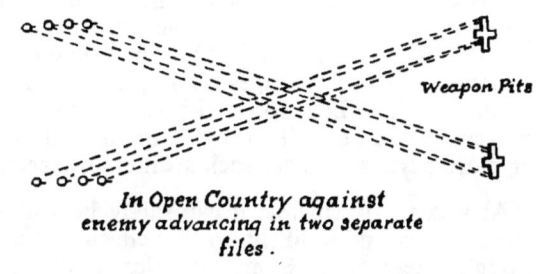

In Open Country against enemy advancing in two separate files.

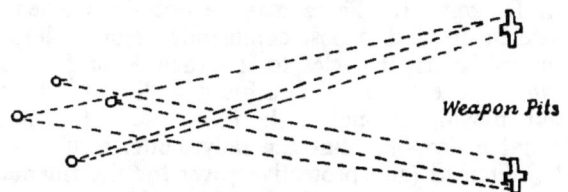

In Open Country against enemy advancing in diamond (or other group) formation.

The Value of Cross-fire *(Continued)*

To obviate the danger of one enemy soldier being hit by three bullets while two others go unharmed, the N.C.O. in command of the firing point should give the range and name the target (using the clock and finger technique prescribed in musketry instruction). At long ranges he may set all his men to fire at the whole force visible, but at shorter ranges he will do well to divide his men into two or more parties, and set each a different target.

As a general principle it can safely be said that cross-fire is more likely to be effective than a straight-ahead aim. Some examples are illustrated in Diagram 1. There may be occasions when a stretch of road is best commanded from a house or wall at right-angles to it. (See *Field Exercise No. 4*, page 105.) Here a heavy or light machine-gun moving through a short traverse is the most suitable weapon. But generally, better results will be obtained (and protective cover for the riflemen or machine-gunners) if two firing points are established one on each side of the road. The diagram shows that a near miss aimed at the first enemy soldier is likely to hit the man behind him.

In open country cross-fire is usually even more profitable. In the diagram two weapon pits are shown, but strong-points, breastworks or ditches would serve equally well. The idea is that the men in each firing-point defend themselves better by firing not at the enemy immediately opposite

TACTICAL RESOURCES AND DISPOSITIONS 37

them, but at the enemy opposite the other firing point. If the enemy is forced to lie down in line abreast the target offered by cross-fire consists not merely of a head and shoulders, but of the whole length of the body. If the enemy advances in a single file midway between the two firing points, cross-fire in the only choice, and the chief advantage here is that the enemy is attacked from both flanks. And if he advances in a diamond or other group formation, cross-fire will almost certainly mean that several of his men at a time come into the sights of a single weapon.

Camouflage.—This is a vexed and contentious subject, but certain principles and technical resources have been devised, and on the essentials there need be no serious dispute.

For Home Guard purposes camouflage is to be regarded as concealment of various subjects (including individuals and bodies of men) from enemy observation. As there is rarely a stable front in modern warfare, concealment must be sought from all sides—including the air.

Three main methods of concealment are in use, and these may be merged into one for a particular purpose. They are:

1. *Blending the object with its background.*—The khaki colour of the British uniform helps to achieve this, and when a soldier lies flat, "takes cover"

behind a dip in the ground, or observes from the middle of a bush he is putting the principle into operation.

2. *Artificial imitation of natural objects.*—The use of turf as a top dressing for the parapet of a weapon pit, and boughs or bracken spread over a firing point or carried on a steel helmet are examples of this method.

3. *Deception.*—An object may be made to look like another more harmless object; for example, a pill-box may be disguised as a shed, or defence works not intended to be occupied may be erected as dummies to draw enemy fire.

4. *Dispersal of forces and adoption of irregular formations.*—A hundred men spread out in small parties are less likely to be observed (and decisively brought under fire) than a hundred grouped together. If the small parties are irregularly disposed, and each adopts a different formation, the concealing effect is increased.

Bodies of men on the move should observe the following rules:

> Whenever possible, move in darkness or in shadow or by covered routes, i.e. through woods, deep lanes, overhung ditches.
>
> At intervals when not on the move and not in complete cover, keep perfectly still. The easiest object to pick out of a landscape (other things being equal) is anything that moves.

TACTICAL RESOURCES AND DISPOSITIONS 39

tree   Stepladder   plank   imitation shell hole
Concealment of Loopholes in a Wall.

Diagram 2
Camouflage

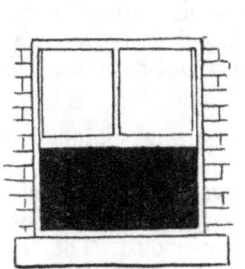

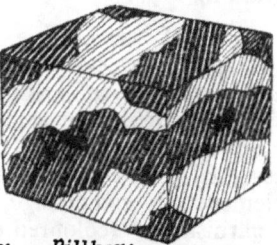

Window firing point:
Room darkened;
No weapons or sandbags showing:

Alternative;
Pull lace curtains across Open window

Pillbox:
Dark bands over loop-holes

Where paint is used for camouflage dark greens, browns and yellows are essential in this country. Darker colours should predominate below and lighter above. More important than colour is texture. Anything which freely reflects light, on vehicles, defence works or personal equipment, is to be avoided. A matt surface is needed.

The familiar camouflage patterns are "disruptive," i.e. they are intended to break up the shape of the object and make its outline difficult to recognise. The pattern must be sweeping and bold, and the darker colour should cover corners and any part of the object which it is important to conceal, e.g. loopholes in a pill-box (see Diagram 2).

Artificial camouflage for strong points and stationary vehicles should be regarded as an additional aid to natural cover. It is futile to spread boughs over a strong point which otherwise stands up naked and obvious. The first essential, and the one which governs all the other elements in camouflage, is the siting. Artificial " garnishing " (coloured canvas strips inserted into nets) is chiefly a foundation, and the vegetation to be found round the site should be used freely on the net. "Garnishing" should be thickest in the centre of the net and thinned out towards the edges.

Positions in open country are easily given away to air observation by smoke from cooking and

TACTICAL RESOURCES AND DISPOSITIONS

tracks made by men approaching them. Tracks should be avoided so far as possible : if this cannot be done, routes must be selected, and adhered to, along the edge of fields and hedges, and false tracks made leading past real positions to a dummy.

Windows in houses used as firing points are best concealed by keeping the weapons and the men to use them far back and by darkening the room itself. If no muzzles protrude and the sandbag breastwork is built two or three feet behind the window (not on or against the sill) little will show. Lace curtains may be left drawn : the men in the room will be able to see through them, but are not visible themselves (see Diagram 2).

Loopholes in walls can best be concealed by siting them in shadow—but shadows move according to the time of day—or by placing some eye-distracting object, such as a plank or a step-ladder, near at hand (see Diagram 2).

Finally, a few hints for individuals.

Keep away from skylines ; find a dip before you raise even your head.

Never cross an open field if you can avoid it : use ditches, hedges, folds in the ground.

Take up a firing position which gives you cover but avoid conspicuous objects such as large trees, sheds, etc., of which the range is easily found.

When not on the move, keep perfectly still.

Seek shadow—and move when the shadow moves.

Facing the sun, keep your head down.

Put your wrist-watch in your pocket and don't carry a white handkerchief in your sleeve.

A dirty face and hands may save your life.

Always approach an occupied position under cover.

Keep the blackout rules very strictly.

Don't carry leaves on your helmet into a ploughed field or a street, or show your leaf-covered helmet against a barn door.

If you use natural vegetation as garnishing, renew it before it fades.

In digging a trench or pit keep the turf aside to cover the parapet.

Tank Traps.—As the essential element in any tank-trap, on which its effectiveness depends, is surprise, this is not a subject to be discussed publicly in great detail. There are plenty of tank-traps involving the use of engineering and ordnance resources not available at present to the Home Guard : these, we may be sure, will be employed by the Regular Army against Nazi advances.

For the Home Guard, however, there is one type, capable of almost infinite variations and local adaptations, which can be used against panzer

TACTICAL RESOURCES AND DISPOSITIONS 43

detachments numbering three to six tanks with motor-cyclist outriders and follow-up infantry in lorries. Experiment has proved its value. The basic idea of this trap is to force the enemy to halt or slow up suddenly in a street lined with houses or in a defile made by roadside banks.

These are the essentials for a tank-trap in a defile:

A. The road must be blocked to resist the advance of the first tank, and the block must be sited round a corner or bend. (In *Field Exercise No.* 4 two blocks are used in the arms of a T road junction.) The aim is to ensure that the main body of the enemy enters the defile before the front tank sights the block and pulls up.

B. This forward road-block must be adequately covered with fire from at least one concealed strong-point (with an alternative position if possible) sited behind, but not usually directly behind, the block, i.e. with the block between them and the enemy. Thus the enemy cannot leave their vehicles on foot to remove the block or overpower the strong-point garrison.

C. Any exits for tanks or infantry from the defile must be stopped and covered with fire.

D. A detachment of the defence should be stationed by the roadside at the end of the defile trap farthest from the forward road block. This detachment must be strong in numbers and armed with weapons appropriate to its various tasks. These tasks are: to erect, if the circumstances permit, another road block in rear of the halted enemy column, but in any event to prevent the column turning or reversing out of the trap; to bring immediate and decisive fire to bear on the follow-up infantry, especially while they are still in their lorry or attempting to descend from it; and, if the infantry are wary, and stay outside the trap, to put out of action any tank or tanks halted near the site of the rear road block. This detachment, therefore, must have comparative strength in numbers. Appropriate arms for it, besides the rifle, are the tommy gun, the light machine-gun, and the close-range anti-tank weapons. It should also carry smoke bombs (see E below) to lob round the lorries and tanks.

E. At points alongside one flank of the defile small parties should be stationed and given two tasks—to destroy the enemy tanks, as soon as they slow up, with close-range anti-tank weapons, and afterwards to pick off with small arms fire the tank crews as they emerge. It is preferable that only one flank of the road be used by these parties to prevent confusion and casualties to comrades; other things being equal, the left flank of the road should be chosen, because from this position a rifle can be fired up the road without the rifleman unduly exposing himself round a wall or the side of a window. These anti-tank parties should also

TACTICAL RESOURCES AND DISPOSITIONS 45

be armed with smoke bombs, and one of these should be lobbed gently on to the road between each pair of tanks, immediately after the first assault. The smoke will add to the confusion of the tank crews, prevent any tanks not immediately disabled from aiming their fire, and the dislodged tank crews will be half blinded as they emerge from the smoke.

F. Long-range anti-tank weapons should be posted at some distance where they can fire their missiles on to any part of the defile. After the first minute they will be aiming at the clouds of smoke.

G. Every man (except perhaps those working the long-range anti-tank weapons) must remain in concealment and under adequate cover. On no account, until the last stages of the operation, must anyone set foot on the road down which machine-guns and long-range anti-tank weapons will be firing. (The order to cease fire should be given to the teams working these weapons by pre-arranged signal.) The enemy, as he enters the trap, should see nothing and hear nothing; the rear road block should be concealed and all firing points camouflaged. But the moment the front tank slows up, action from all points should be simultaneous and decisive.

H. If the most suitable defile is too short to contain the full enemy column, a variation of this scheme can be employed at the forward road block. The motor-cyclist outriders should be allowed to pass the block (camouflaged or covered) and round the next bend on the road, a wire hawser, at the height of a man's hips, should suddenly be hauled up in front of them. They will be forced to jam on their brakes, and should then be picked off by marksmen stationed near at hand. As soon as the motor cyclists are disposed of, the marksmen should reinforce the garrison of the strong-points covering the road block.

The fate of the motor-cyclists, round the bend of the road, is neither known nor suspected by the enemy tanks following them, who are duly halted by the road-block. The closing of this road-block, after the motor-cyclists have passed, must be done swiftly and may involve risks to the man detailed for the task. These risks must be taken. Very often, however, local ingenuity with ropes, chains and other improvised instruments, should make it possible for the block or its essential parts to be hauled across the road by a small party concealed at the side.

I. The operation of such a tank-trap as this is planned to meet an enemy detachment proceeding in the order used by the Nazis in France and the Low Countries. In the meantime, however, the enemy may have revised his ideas. He may, for example, prefer to send his motor-cyclists a quarter or half a mile ahead. In this event they must be disposed of separately, and all traces of them removed from view, the tank-trap garrisons immediately going back to their stations. He may use one tank for reconnaisance : if so, the defence commander must decide either to let it go through and fall on it elsewhere, in order to catch the main body of tanks, or to destroy it and hope to remove or conceal it before the others arrive. Such activities are inevitably subject to air observation and a detachment should be given the task of attempting to bring down any enemy plane flying very low ; apart from this, the concealment of the garrison and the postponement of road-block erection till the last safe moment should thwart air observation. Another variation which the enemy may use is to send his lorry-borne infantry, with or without motor cyclist outriders, in advance of his tanks, which he is likely to regard as more valuable. The only decision here is to catch them in the trap and destroy them. The tanks following up will in any event be much more vulnerable without infantry support.

Street Fighting.—Street fighting is a complicated operation difficult to plan and to control. For the Home Guard it may take place immediately after the holding up of the enemy vehicles in a defile or may be part of the resistance to his attempt to occupy a town or village by infantry attack. It does not follow that the Home Guard rôle will be purely defensive: the enemy may have to be driven out of positions he has seized, or he may take refuge in houses when he finds himself cornered.

In street fighting deployment is usually impossible: each side must work in small parties, usually proceeding in single file, and, indeed, it will be the endeavour of both to keep out of the street, taking up positions inside buildings or fighting a way from building to building or room to room. Reconnaissance and communications are exceptionally difficult. The area to be defended should therefore be reconnoitred thoroughly now, inside buildings as well as outside, and sections and squads should be trained to act independently. The searching of houses must be done systematically: if possible, entry should be made from the roof and the house cleared, floor by floor, downwards. Otherwise the order is: ground floor, basement, cellars, then the first and upper floors. A guard should be left in the hall, and the searcher covered by another man with weapon ready.

In certain areas the Home Guard will form part of the town or city defence scheme, and their operations, including the fortification of houses, will follow the standard regulations. Camouflage, including the concealment of loopholes and the darkening of rooms behind them, is most important for street fighting. Tanks are at a serious disadvantage in streets and directed artillery fire is

TACTICAL RESOURCES AND DISPOSITIONS 49

not very probable. But dive bombing and random air bombardments are among the difficulties the defence must expect to encounter. If gas or smoke is used by the enemy his intention will probably be to hold the defenders in position while his main body passes elsewhere. It is also very likely that he will use various incendiary weapons. The Home Guard therefore must be prepared to hold its defences stubbornly, but also to put into effect at short notice the principle of Local Mobility, moving quickly to alternative positions by previously reconnoitred routes under cover.

Almost every Home Guard weapon can be used in street fighting: the rifle and bayonet for searches, machine-guns for commanding a stretch of road, grenades and tommy-guns for house-to-house fighting, smoke bombs for confusing the enemy, and all the anti-tank weapons for assaulting the vehicles in which he may approach.

Fortified buildings should have outer defences of barbed wire covering weapon-pits, with communication trenches back to the building. Cellars should be strengthened, made gas-proof, and used for storing ammunition and supplies. The ground floor should generally be used for small arms fire, and upper floors for grenades, anti-tank weapons, observation and visual signalling. Fire-fighting apparatus should be at hand on each floor.

Patrols.—Patrols should be organised so that

each member performs a different and specific function. This secures the maximum effectiveness and provides all-round protection against surprise. The first man looks to his front as he proceeds, and is ready to fire in that direction. The next man looks to the left, and the third to the right. A rear-guard of two walking backwards most of the time, or halting, if the patrol is on all fours, from time to time to cover the rear, is essential. Diagram 3 shows the disposition of such a patrol for the country or along an open road. At night the patrol is wider spread but not so deep.

A street patrol needs more men because its observation will be limited by the houses, and it is more likely to be fired on at short range. The patrol must proceed in sub-divisions on both sides of the road. One pair on the left will observe and be ready to fire on the houses (all floors) on the opposite side of the street. The following pair, on the right, will act similarly against the side of the street down which the first pair are moving. Thus each covers the other. The rear-guard needs an extra man to cover them against surprise from the front, i.e. their rear. (See Diagram 3.)

Note: on no account should a patrol enter any defile other than a street. A natural defile should be reconnoitred from the banks and with great care.

Alternatives in Emergency.—All good tactical movements are simple and sound, and both

TACTICAL RESOURCES AND DISPOSITIONS 51

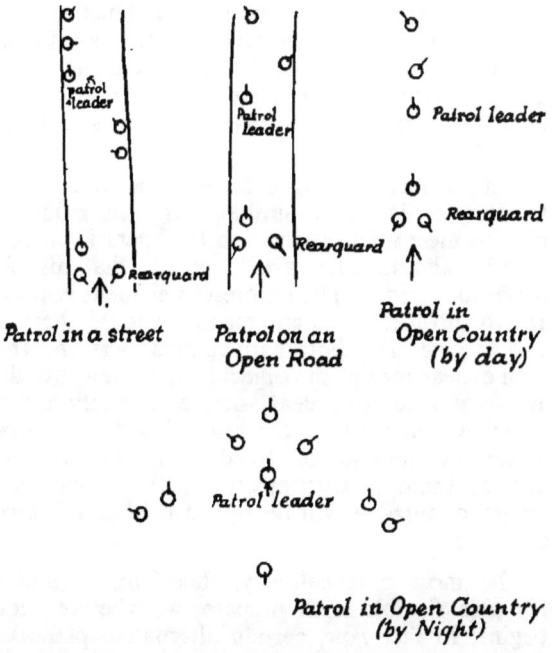

Diagram 3   Formation of Patrols

commanders and the men they command should be trained in them until it becomes instinctive to do the right thing to meet each situation as it arises and changes. Weapon training should merge into field exercises, and be tested by them. The use of weapon-training officers as umpires is especially valuable.

But tactical training can never become a drill. Uniformity is not desirable. And in making a plan to meet a given situation the operational commander should take care to ensure that his plan is not too rigid. The unforeseen element is always apt to intrude. The commander should therefore aim to give his subordinate commanders and their men a clear idea of the object or main purpose they are to pursue, and clear, simple instructions how to achieve it, while at the same time leaving them a certain amount of freedom in the carrying out of these instructions. On the other hand, no good purpose will be served if he is indecisive or vague.

The most practical way, therefore, of making his plan flexible is to prepare, well before action begins, in fact *now*, certain alternative plans and train every man in the unit to understand that these alternatives may be used under orders of the commander on the spot.

First: fire positions in defence works or covering road blocks should be duplicated, though not

TACTICAL RESOURCES AND DISPOSITIONS 53

necessarily in the same material. Thus, if one becomes untenable for any reason, another is immediately available.

Second: where sections or squads are most likely to have to move in contact or prospective contact with the enemy, alternative lines for advance and withdrawal should be worked out and tested in field exercises. Where a withdrawal is necessary, it should be conducted along either of the alternative lines, on the principle: " Before letting go in front, hold fast behind." This means that outposts should withdraw through or round posts in their rear which are manned and able to afford them covering fire. If the rear posts are not already manned, a detachment from the outposts must be sent back to hold them before the withdrawal begins. (See *Field Exercise No. 2*, page 93).

Third, however determined a commander may be to hold his position in the face of the enemy, he should remember that circumstances (air bombardment, gas, smoke or orders from higher authority), may compel him to vacate it temporarily. To meet this situation he should make known to every man under his command two alternative rallying points outside his inner defences. These rallying points should be in concealment and under cover. Standing orders should specify one to be tried first, then the other.

In making a way to them men should move cautiously and reconnoitre to make sure the enemy has not already forestalled them. The first men to arrive at a rallying point should prepare it as a defensive position and put out sentries to challenge.

CHAPTER III

SOME SPECIAL PROBLEMS

Local Mobility.—Every unit of the Home Guard has its own prepared defences designed to cover vital points or to obstruct the passage of the enemy. These Home Guard defences are part of the national defence system, and very often are closely interlocked with Regular Army defences. Because of these facts it may fairly be asked how the new principle of Local Mobility (replacing the earlier Static Defence) is to be applied.

No single answer can be given to this question. Everything depends on local circumstances. But this much may be safely said: every Home Guard commander needs to study and organise a system of swift and variable transport routes in his own district. Normally his men will not leave that area, but within it the more efficiently he can move men and weapons the greater will be his power of resistance and attack.

Here are some of the reasons, and most commanders will find one or other of them applicable to his own case.

A. The exact direction of the enemy's approach cannot be fore-known. He has a fondness for pincers and outflanking movements. He may therefore seek to avoid the prepared defences, to pass by them on a flank at no cost to himself. The commander must take account of these possibilities in defining his object and making plans to achieve it. If the orders given him by higher authority, and the resources at his disposal, permit he may be able to leave an adequate garrison in the prepared defences while a striking force is assembled and transported to the nearest point whence it can attack the enemy on the move and at least harass and delay him.

B. It is not always possible for a Home Guard Commander to dispose a sufficient number of men to block every feasible route of enemy approach. Nevertheless, he will be well advised to form a small reserve at his battle headquarters, composed of active and well trained men, and supplied with as large a variety of weapons as possible. This reserve should be regarded as a striking force. Speedy transport should always be available, possibly a car may be armour-plated and mounted with a machine-gun (see page 58). The reserve can be thrown in with decisive effect to reinforce a hard-pressed defence or to enfilade the enemy from a flank or to strike at an air-borne landing. And where a unit has to guard three or more approaches and the enemy attack develops on one, it may be advisable, after despatching this motorised reserve, temporarily to deplete the garrisons in the

SOME SPECIAL PROBLEMS 57

other approaches and so quickly form a second and temporary reserve. (See *Field Exercise* No. 9, page 132.)

C. For various reasons the prepared defences may become untenable for a time. If this occurs, the motorised reserve may—dependent on time and topographical factors—be able to cover the withdrawal of the garrisons on foot or by bicycle.

D. The enemy may halt outside the prepared defences and deploy his follow-up infantry to attack from the flanks. The motorised reserve can then be rushed by road to the most suitable point for meeting this attack. This will spare valuable time for any re-organisation of the defence garrisons which may be necessary.

Motor transport is obviously the most suitable instrument for achieving Local Mobility, but alternative preparations should be made in case the cars and lorries are damaged or run short of petrol, or the roads are blocked by bomb craters and debris. Every available bicycle should be mobilised. Motor transport for the Home Guard must move in small groups in order not to block roads needed for the movement of regular troops or to expose itself over much to air attack. And precautions must be taken to prevent any and every form of transport falling into the hands of the enemy.

If the enemy is pursued or hard pressed he must be attacked with full power where he is. If he attempts to make airborne landings outside the prepared defences, every man and weapon which can be spared must be rushed to the scene of the landing. If he is moving by road or across country he must be intercepted. The aim of the Home Guard Commander should be to drive the enemy into open country and to keep him there, denying him the use of the roads while taking full advantage of them for the Home Guard. Thus Local Mobility should primarily be regarded as a means of getting men and weapons to the scene of probable action. In certain areas the formation of a Company Reserve as a motorised striking force is advisable and—where higher authority permits—one or two cars may be armour-plated from local resources. Concrete an inch thick, with revetment wire as reinforcement, between thin plates, gives good protection. All plating should slope inwards to deflect enemy fire. Apart from this, the aim of the Home Guard attacking the enemy on the move should be to get into firing positions, concealed and protected, across the line of his advance or on a flank. They should then let him come unsuspectingly well into range, and open fire on him with surprising and devastating effect.

Small Arms Weapons.—" Small arms " has become a slightly misleading expression : it would perhaps be nearer the mark to speak of " small calibre "—calibre being the internal diameter of the tube or barrel through which the missile is

SOME SPECIAL PROBLEMS 59

projected. For Home Guard purposes, at least, the following can be classified as small arms weapons: the rifle: the automatic rifle or light machine gun: the medium and heavy machine gun: the sub-machine gun (tommy gun): the revolver; the shot gun firing a special charge.

They are all to be regarded as pre-eminently anti-personnel weapons; i.e., to be directed against men, not machines. There are a few exceptions to this generalisation, which must be taken strictly as exceptions. Machine guns, especially heavy machine guns, can and should be used against low-flying aircraft as a suitable occasion arises. The aeroplane in flight is a difficult target and ammunition should not be wasted. Dive-bombers should not be fired on unless and until they come very close in attacking a machine-gun post. Planes carrying parachutists fly very low and slow for some time. They should be attacked but with a maximum range of two hundred yards. Good fire-control is essential. No small arms weapon, however, should be used against a troop-carrying glider: even if the fabric or structure is riddled, a crash is not likely to result; once the glider has landed it ceases to be a mobile target and the troops it carries can be brought under concentrated fire. The same argument makes it a waste of time and ammunition to fire at parachutes; the target should be the parachutist just landed or landing. The only other occasion when a small arms weapon can be profitably used other than against men is when a tank or other armoured vehicle is halted and—at close range—it is possible to aim accurately at the vents. Shots at members of a tank crew showing their heads through an opened turret count as anti-personnel fire.

Because this has become largely a war of machines there is in some quarters a tendency to undervalue small arms weapons, particularly the rifle. It is true to say that aircraft and tanks provide—so far as we can foresee—the most formidable elements in the Nazi invasion plan. It is true also that unless and until we can put those machines out of action the small arms weapons of the Home Guard are not likely to be of much use. But we have plans and techniques for dealing with those machines.—See *Tank Traps*, p. 42). And if we look at the problem from the other point of view, the Nazi point of view, we shall see that they do not by any means rely on machines alone.

Every Nazi tank section moving independently is likely to be protected by motor cyclists (i.e., mounted infantry) and follow-up infantry transported in lorries: their task will be to deploy, outflank and overcome any local resistance which may hold up the tanks or threaten them with disaster. In addition, the panzer columns, landed from the air or the sea, will be aided by air-borne

SOME SPECIAL PROBLEMS 61

troops, sent over by parachute and glider or troop-carrying plane. Once landed, these air-borne troops will act as infantry detachments—aided probably by light tanks and artillery. Again, the Nazis know perfectly well that panzer columns and infantry detachments dropped from the air will not suffice to conquer and hold down even a part of this country. They will try to land large forces of occupying troops.

All these offer targets to small arms fire, and targets which must not be missed if the invasion is to be defeated.

No Home Guardsman, therefore, need fear he is carrying round a weapon which he will not be able to use effectively. But he must use it with a thorough understanding of what it can and cannot do. He should make himself master of its mechanism and learn to handle it with the confident ease of familiarity. From time to time he should test himself in all the elements of its use, especially aiming and trigger pressure. He should use field exercises incidentally as a test of his weapon-training and as practice in keeping a cool and intelligent head on his shoulders, obeying orders strictly and promptly, finding the right thing to do when no orders are forthcoming. If his post is in a firing point, covering a road block, for example, he will remember that even in moments of high excitement he must not waste ammunition on the armour-plating of tanks: his business is to look for heads showing through open turrets, crews emerging from damaged or burning tanks, infantry in their lorries or leaving the lorries or deployed off the road.

The automatic rifle is to be regarded primarily as a single shot weapon. Each shot can be aimed at an individual mark, but the automatic recocking and ejection of the spent cartridge means that an exceptionally high rate of rapid fire can be achieved. There will be few occasions for a prolonged burst of fire—but one of them is when lorry-borne infantry come into the sights. Normally, a series of short bursts, with the trigger pressed only for a second or two, is more effective in firing at groups of the enemy than the continuous expenditure of a whole magazine.

The automatic rifle as a weapon against low-flying aircraft (and they should be flying very low) is best used from a trench or ditch, or with the rifleman flat on his back. The Lewis gun and the heavy machine gun can hardly be used in this way against aircraft. Special mountings are necessary. The shaft should be extensible and a lock provided to clamp it in the extended position, yet giving free play. The ideal to aim at is a stand which will enable the gun to be swung to bring fire to bear in any direction, and at short or long ranges, on ground targets, while the extension converts the gun in a

SOME SPECIAL PROBLEMS 63

second or two into an anti-aircraft weapon. Another idea worth consideration is to bore the splayed feet of the tripod to take a bolt. A number of lorries likely to be available in the event of action can then be prepared, and the tripod with the gun can then be mounted on whichever of the lorries first comes to hand when it is needed. A lorry so fitted can be used for the transport of reserves (Local Mobility), and the machine-gun team can use it as a platform, firing from behind road blocks or moving round by a circuitous route to take the lorry-borne enemy infantry from a flank.

Tommy-guns should be regarded as deadly weapons for close-range fighting. Because their range is so short they should be fired only in brief bursts, especially as in such fighting it will not always be easy to exchange magazines. The shotgun, loaded with its special ammunition, can also have a terrific effect at short range—but cover should be obtained because of the time needed for reloading.

The bayonet for most Home Guard purposes is essentially a weapon for sentries and night patrols. Bayonet fighting should therefore be taught with this restricted aim in view. Home Guard formations in urban areas may usefully add practice in bayonet work for street fighting and house searching.

Anti-Tank Weapons.—In order to preserve secrecy and add to the effect of the unpleasant surprises awaiting the invader, only those weapons which were in general use before the outbreak of war may be described or even named in public print. No one will question the wisdom of this ruling. Since the L.D.V. days when Molotoff cocktails were first made and tested in this country, a sizable range of anti-tank weapons has become available for the Home Guard. Those units which are stationed in areas regarded as most vulnerable are supplied first, but it can safely be said that very soon after this book is published (if not before) every Home Guard formation will have several of these new and secret weapons among its armaments. Nor will it be long before the whole range—some items of which are exclusive to the Home Guard, so that supplies will not be held up while deliveries are made to the full-time Army—is available for every unit.

Some of the tactical uses to which these secret anti-tank weapons may be put are discussed in these pages. All that can otherwise be said about them is that they fall into two main categories—explosive and incendiary. Or, from another point of view, they can be sub-divided as: short-range anti-tank weapons, to be lobbed on to or under tanks, and discharged on contact or by hand release; and long-range anti-tank weapons which are missiles projected from some distance. Commanders may think it worth while to consider the mounting of these long-range weapons on cars, with or without armour, as suggested for machine-guns.

SOME SPECIAL PROBLEMS 65

But a final word about the Molotoff: this incendiary weapon is by no means to be despised. During one of the Nazi attacks on Tobruk three of the tanks which for a time penetrated the perimeter defences were destroyed by Molotoffs.

Gas Warfare.—Because the enemy has restrained himself from the use of gas for so long it is not to be assumed that he will do so if and when he decides to attempt an invasion. Gas is not a decisive but an auxiliary weapon of war, and is most likely to be employed to cause confusion, panic and the immobility of forces which might otherwise move against the enemy. It may be sprayed from the air, either from a great altitude or from very low overhead. It may be sent in shells or in bombs from planes. Or it may be discharged in clouds to be carried by the wind, from containers established on shore or kept on vessels off the coast.

Gas may be used in one of several main classifications: it may affect the nose, the eyes, the skin, or the skin and throat; or it may combine several or all of these properties. Some gases are odourless and the first effect by which they can be recognised is a headache and emotional depression. Against all these varieties of gas—which, so far as research can foresee, cover all possibilities—the officially-issued respirators, eye-shades and ointments afford complete protection.

Gas is a tricky and two-edged weapon. German troops will not be anxious to pass through areas subjected to German gas. Moreover, the use of gas invites immediate reprisals, and the nation which decides on this step must (apart from any moral questions) be sure that its own home population is adequately protected and not likely to panic.

The situation can therefore be summed up thus: it is a possibility, but not a probability, that the Nazis will use gas against this country. The two strong deterrents are its limited and temporary effectiveness and the likelihood of reprisals having a disastrous effect on the German population at home.

If, however, gas is used as an adjunct to an attempted invasion, no one in this country who uses his equipment promptly and keeps calm is likely to suffer. Home Guard commanders, however, should remember that if gas is used against their units it will in all probability mean that the enemy hopes to cause confusion there and restrict activity. They should be prepared to put into effect the principle of Local Mobility and make use of alternative positions already prepared.

Fire-Fighting.—It is most important that Home Guardsmen should be trained to deal with incendiary bombs and the fires they cause. By doing this they will not merely aid civil defence before

SOME SPECIAL PROBLEMS 67

and during an invasion, but enable themselves to hold fortified houses and other positions which otherwise would become untenable.

The subject of fire-fighting is complicated and should be studied in some detail. But these are the essentials which must be covered :

1. *Recognition of Incendiary Bombs.*—These may be of various sizes and weights. The commonest is the magnesium bomb, weighing about two pounds. The colour is that of aluminium, with which the magnesium is alloyed. It contains a primer which burns for forty to fifty seconds, and ignites the aluminium-magnesium of which practically the whole bomb consists. The heat is intense—1,300 degrees Centigrade. The base is blunt to ensure that the bomb does not penetrate far below the roof. Up to two thousand of these can be dropped from one heavy bomber—singly, in line, from a container (bread-basket) or in groups. Other types are the thermite and the phosphorous —not so effective—and the petrol bomb.

2. *The use of the Sandbag and Stirrup Handpump.*—Bombs which fall in the street can be left for the time being. Large bombs should be dealt with by the fire brigade or A.F.S. When incendiaries are dropped, fire-fighters must search every building in their care, beginning with the attics and roof. Some bombs contain explosives, which go off after they have been burning for a time.

All bombs, therefore, should be approached with care, and the face and shoulders protected by a half-filled sandbag held in front. The sandbag should be dropped over the bomb. This will not put it out; it will burn through a wooden floor very quickly. Another man should inspect the ceiling of the floor below and place a bucket of sand underneath; caught in this, the bomb will burn itself out harmlessly.

Because of the great heat generated and the smoke—as well as the explosive—an incendiary bomb should be approached in a crawling position. If floors have been weakened by fire, crawl close to the walls. This is also the surest way of finding the door in a room filled with smoke. The door of a burning room should be kept closed, or nearly closed, to prevent a draught increasing the fire. In opening a door, first place one foot three inches from the opening edge; the hot gases from a burning bomb may set up a terrific pressure of air, and on the handle being turned the door may burst open violently.

The stirrup pump should be used principally to put out the fire caused by the bomb, and not the bomb itself, which cannot be extinguished by water. Indeed, if the *jet* from the pump is directed on the bomb it may spread the incendiary material. Three men make the team to work the pump. No. 1 goes to the fire. No. 2 follows with the pump and bucket, and then works the stirrup and handle while No. 1 crawls towards the fire holding the nozzle above his head and directing the *jet* on to the boards, curtains, furniture or fire, and from time to time directing the *spray* (jet and spray are controlled by a pushbutton on the nozzle) at the bomb; this may prevent any explosive charge in the bomb going off, and will certainly make the bomb burn itself out quicker. No. 3 is a general utility and stand-by man, to refill buckets and to go to the floor below to place a bucket of sand underneath where the bomb may burn its way through.

If the bomb is found immediately, it may be lifted with a long-handled shovel into a bucket of sand. Otherwise it is not safe to approach even from a distance until the bomb is known to have burned for two minutes. If by that time it has not exploded it may be regarded as a simple incendiary.

No. 1 on the stirrup pump has a difficult job and should protect his face as much as possible behind a sandbag.

CHAPTER IV

FIELD EXERCISES AND LEADERSHIP

NEXT to instruction and practice in the use of weapons, field exercises form the most important part of Home Guard training. This applies to town and city units as much as to those with stretches of open country to defend. The term "field exercise" should be taken to mean any mimic operation of war involving the use of a substantial proportion of a platoon, whether it is conducted over moors, meadows, woods and hillsides, or in built-up areas.

The field exercise can be made to serve several valuable purposes. It should give Home Guardsmen practice in what are likely to be their duties if and when the Germans are able to make war by land in this country; it should enable them to test unpredictably, spontaneously and in circumstances continually changing, all the otherwise unco-ordinated details of soldiering they have been taught. Thus a series of field exercises offers opportunities for more or less realistic practice in the use of the various Home Guard weapons, in fire control, range finding, correct aim and trigger pressure (under conditions very different from the rifle range), as well as in camouflage, taking cover,

FIELD EXERCISES AND LEADERSHIP

accurate observation and report, movement under fire, sniping and ambushes.

The limitations of the field exercise are obvious. It cannot reproduce the noise, the nerve strain, the casualties and the confusion of actual battle. But within these limits it should be made as realistic as possible. The Home Guard should, for most if not all field exercises, operate as a whole in the unit or sub-unit which is most likely to act more or less independently under invasion conditions. Thus in some districts the platoon will furnish the whole of the attack or defence; in others, the company. It should never be forgotten, however, that even where comparatively large numbers are available, the success of any operation largely depends on the section, which itself may at any time have to act independently. Section leaders should be chosen with great care, encouraged and consulted, and trained in all the qualities of leadership. In cities and large towns it may be possible to bring a whole battalion under single operational control. This means that a neighbouring platoon (or company or battalion) must be asked to co-operate, furnishing for the day attack against defence or vice versa. In many districts regular troops stationed near at hand will gladly join in a field exercise. And often Air Force units will supply the most realistic element of all, in the form of dive-bombing and low machine-gunning flights. For smaller scale field exercises, which

72 ADVANCED TRAINING FOR HOME GUARD

can be more easily and quickly arranged, one section can be set against three, or two against two. But practice for the operational unit acting as a whole, under single control, is the true end to be achieved.

The aim of the officer or officers preparing a field exercise should generally be to provide the two opposing commanders with such information and such specific orders that there is a reasonable probability of the two forces making early contact. Under the conditions of actual warfare such contacts are not always easy to achieve, but in field exercises it is worth while taking the trouble to make them probable: otherwise valuable hours are wasted and keen men are left with a feeling of frustration. The exercise should set definite topographical, time and operational limits with this purpose in view. But the two commanders should not receive more specific information about each other's intentions, forces and dispositions, than they are likely to get under actual conditions of war, and once zero hour arrives everything should be left to them to decide. Where prepared defences are to be attacked, there is rarely any trouble in ensuring contact, but where both forces are mobile, and the exact dispositions of each improvised and necessarily unknown to the other at the beginning of the exercise, the most satisfactory method in preparing the exercise is to ensure that one section of the attack traverses a limited area which is given

FIELD EXERCISES AND LEADERSHIP 73

to one section of the defence to guard. If a a penetration is effected, or the attackers are utterly surprised, the responsibility can afterwards be placed either on the commander for faulty dispositions or on the subordinate commander on the spot for tactical deficiencies.

This indicates another essential for a satisfactory field exercise—a sufficient number of umpires. In general terms it can be laid down that there should be one umpire present with each sub-unit—the section, if the platoon is the operational unit, the platoon if the company acts as a whole. If there are fewer umpires than this, disputes are inevitable: each side believes that it opened fire first and inflicted heavy casualties at no cost to itself. At best, the men feel that their good work has been wasted because no independent judge was present to observe. Umpires should wear a prominent mark (such as a white handkerchief on the sleeve or shoulder strap) to distinguish them from the combatants. It is an advantage, though not an essential, if they can be drawn from outside the membership of the units taking part. Higher commanders and officers on the staff at H.Q., (weapons-training, intelligence, pioneer officers, etc.) are valuable as umpires not only because of their prestige but because they bring specialist knowledge with them. And occasionally an exchange of umpires between adjacent platoons, companies or battalions is helpful: it promotes liaison, and the experience of seeing another unit at work often suggests new ideas and discovers unsuspected deficiencies in the training of one's own.

A well planned and efficiently carried out exercise affords instruction and enjoyment to everyone concerned, but care must be taken that, owing to exuberance and the absence of live ammunition, the operation does not degenerate into a display of high spirits. Some commanders like to let their men finish up with a wild charge at the enemy " because they enjoy it." In my view this is a most dangerous practice and should always be avoided. Such charging, in the Royal Academy picture manner, usually results in heavy casualties, and what men practise in mimic warfare they are apt to carry out when they meet a real enemy— that is indeed the whole aim of weapon-training and field exercises. Close-quarter fighting should never occur (except by night or in the undergrowth of woods) unless a genuine surprise is effected— and then a post-mortem is called for to discover why and how one side was surprised.

The natural keenness of men and commanders can be relied on to overcome a good deal of the non-realist atmosphere of field exercises, but care should be taken that this keenness does not lead to men moving about incautiously, rushing past gaps in hedges bunched together, showing themselves on the skyline to gain the advantage of speed, merely because they know that on this occasion they are not going to be penalised by bullets. Umpires should be ever present and ever vigilant to award casualties against indiscretions. It also helps to achieve the air of realism if umpires (by previous arrangement and at a certain stage in the operations) intervene to produce a drastic and sudden change in the situation beyond what might normally be expected from the opposing force. Thus at a certain point an umpire might go to the local commander and say to him: "The enemy has brought up a gun and is pumping gas shells (or smoke bombs) into your defences. What are you going to do about it?" Alternatively he might say: "Three Spitfires have come down low and are machine-gunning the enemy attacking you. Now get on with it." Or again: "You have been dive-bombed. You yourself are out of action and twenty of your men. Your strong point is untenable." After that, the umpire would observe who carries on and how.

Some Home Guard units are responsible for the defence of areas comparatively large in relation to the forces at their disposal. This should be regarded not as a handicap but as an advantage. Even those units which are charged with the duty of holding prepared defences at all costs should remember that circumstances (especially perhaps dive-bombing, gas, and smoke screens) or a change of general orders as the major military situation alters may force them to leave these prepared defences at any rate for a time. It is the duty of the commander to prepare his men by field exercises for such eventualities. The role of the Home Guard has been defined as Static Warfare—an unfortunate phrase—but this should not be taken with too strict a literalness. There are alternative ways of defending towns and villages besides waiting behind inner defences for the enemy to attack.

In general, Static Defence means that each Home Guard unit will operate only on its own territory, but on that territory it should cultivate Local Mobility to the utmost degree of speed, flexibility and striking power. This means that every point to be defended should be covered by a number of alternative positions, well concealed, and if possible connected by covered approaches. It also means that men should be conveyed by road to the nearest feasible point whence they can attack the enemy, thus saving time and fatigue.

Field exercises offer an invaluable opportunity for the practice of Local Mobility, and, so far as petrol supplies allow, motor transport should be used in the exercises themselves. Bicycles make the next best substitute. The blocking of roads by bomb craters and debris, however, should be allowed for, and care should be taken that motor transport is not incautiously parked where its presence may give away even the most carefully concealed position.

FIELD EXERCISES AND LEADERSHIP

The fighting function of the Home Guard must not be allowed to obscure or hinder its duty to observe and report (by the authorised means) all enemy movements. This is an essential part of every well-planned exercise, and on no account is it to be omitted. Every member of the unit should be practised in the duties of the scout and runner, and headquarters staff should take it in turn to receive and transmit messages. From time to time umpires should announce that telephone communications have broken down, and not merely platoon commanders and section leaders but the men entrusted with messages should be left to meet the situation out of their own resources.

Finally, one of the most valuable aspects of the field exercise is that it affords commanders and seconds-in-command experience in the operational control of their units (ranging in size down to the section or even a squad of seven or eight men) in making dispositions and plans on the ground they can expect to fight over, and to some extent in testing by trial and error the active service efficiency of themselves and the men under their control. It would be too much to ask that every commander in the Home Guard should possess the experience and ability of a first-class general. Yet an outline knowledge of the broad principles of successful modern land warfare is essential. Such an outline knowledge must remain academic unless and until it is fully absorbed and understood. These principles need not be studied in detail, but they should—indeed they must—become the basis of all the commander's thinking and decisions.

After the penetrative power and speed of movement of the armoured division with air support—and arising out of it—the development which most strikingly distinguishes the warfare of to-day from that of 1914–18 is the impossibility of the higher command retaining close control over the activities of its units once action has started. With certain reservations, it was true to say that in 1914–18 a divisional commander could operate three or four brigades of infantry together with supporting artillery, engineers, supply and medical services. That rarely holds good to-day. The division has reduced its numbers (but increased its fire-power and its mobility) and must often work in smaller, separated, independent parts. Every subaltern, indeed every sergeant of infantry, is now trained to take up the responsibilities of independent command on occasion and for indefinite periods.

What is true of the rest of the Army is even more applicable to the Home Guard. The size of the operational unit varies with the density of population and the permanent or temporary presence of regular troops, but in general it can be said that every platoon commander and section-leader (and his second-in-command) must be prepared to act as an independent commander, making his own

FIELD EXERCISES AND LEADERSHIP

appreciations and decisions on the spot. In brief, he must be ready to fulfil the role of a general, if only for a limited time. To do this efficiently he needs to cultivate clear thinking and obtain a grasp of certain basic principles which will direct all his military preparations and actions.

These principles can be stated quite simply. The problem is to apply them in times of stress, when exact and true knowledge is hard to come by, and difficult to distinguish from rumour, exaggeration and false or irrelevant reports. The more frequent, and the more realistic practice the commander can obtain before he finds himself confronted with the real and befogged problems of modern war, the better for him, for the Home Guard, and the country.

As a basis for every operational plan, the commander should cultivate, until it becomes a habit and instinct, the device of imagining himself into the position of the enemy. The first question must always be: " What would I do if I were the Nazi commander with a Nazi background and outlook, and Nazi forces at my disposal ? " And here the Nazi principle of speed reinforced by terror, possibly careless of casualties to its own side, must be borne in mind. The enemy's probable purpose once established, the Home Guard plan must be designed to defeat it.

These, then, are the principles on which it can safely be said that good leadership is based.

1. *The commander must know, and never forget, his main object.*

Note first that the military "object" means purpose or aim. It should not be confused with "objective" which signifies a place or line of country to be reached.

The object of Home Guard operations may vary considerably. It may be to prevent the enemy reaching one or more places in the unit area; it may be to observe and report the enemy's movements and keep contact with him: it may be to keep the enemy out of a town or village by manning strong points: or to observe, report and oppose the landing of air-borne troops: or to cut off a cross-country movement: to deny the enemy the use of a railway: or to fight his tanks and follow-up infantry (at a place selected beforehand by the Home Guard): or to facilitate the passage of our own troops: or to defend a factory or airfield: or it may be some combination of these.

To a certain extent the probable nature of these objects can be foreseen now, but surprises by the enemy should be allowed for. Until he receives information from his own scouts or from other reliable sources the commander acting independently cannot finally determine what his object will be. His standing orders and defence plans will define for him his object in general terms, from which he must never depart. Once he

FIELD EXERCISES AND LEADERSHIP 81

receives information of an enemy approach he should be able to define his object in greater detail, first to himself, then his subordinate commanders. He, and they, then know the object (or main purpose) in view. Everything that follows is a means of attaining that end.

2. *The commander must make his plan for attaining his object conform to the forces and weapons at his disposal.*

The Home Guard cannot afford to miss any genuine opportunity of opposing, hindering and inflicting casualties on the enemy. Speed of action is all important. Orders must be given quickly and clearly. But keenness is no excuse for initiating an operation unless there is a reasonable prospect of carrying it to a successful conclusion. (If orders are received from a higher authority, that is another matter; they must be obeyed immediately and fully. Here we are concerned only with the commander who has to exercise an independent command.)

As soon as he has imagined himself in the place of the enemy, and calculated the enemy's purpose, the commander can make his own plan. He will then quickly consider whether he has sufficient men, sufficient time, and sufficient fire power to give him a reasonable chance of bringing it to a successful conclusion. If not, he must reject that plan and find another one more feasible. He should not order an offensive operation, for example, if he cannot get enough men in contact with the enemy in time. He should not attack tanks with machine guns, rifles and grenades unless he can first halt them or slow them down and dislodge the tank crews. But Local Mobility is to be reckoned among his resources. So long as he can break off action and renew it from another place and in a different way, he may be justified in attacking swiftly even though he is not fully informed of the enemy strength.

3. *The commander must try to surprise the enemy, to do what the enemy does not expect.*

In order to achieve surprise—a most valuable element in any operation—the commander must exercise his imagination with energy and good sense. He must put himself in the place of the enemy arriving in the locality by air, land or sea, with no more knowledge of the district than is to be gained from maps and perhaps photographs. He should try to realise the purposes which the enemy is likely to carry out and the difficulties confronting him. He must try hard for a few moments to think as a Nazi would think. Then, returning to his own point of view, he should seek to thwart the enemy purpose in ways the enemy will least expect and least relish. In particular, he should be ready to exploit such difficulties as the enemy

FIELD EXERCISES AND LEADERSHIP 83

is not likely to discover until he has rubbed his nose up against them.

There may be sound reasons why the commander should choose obvious lines and methods of attack and defence. But where alternative courses of approximately equal promise are open, it is wise to choose the one which—from the enemy's point of view—is less likely to be foreseen and forestalled. If, for example, a potential landing-ground can be brought under fire from a bridge, from a ditch or from a spinney, it might be well to choose the ditch, remembering that it is not so prominent on the map nor so visible from ground level. At the same time, the other two firing points might be used by smaller parties to distract the enemy's attention while the main attack develops. If nearby villages have their defences placed close within the village, it might pay the commander to give battle outside his own village. Or he might furnish two or three dummy defences or traps in succession, and use the next position along the enemy's line of advance to surprise him just as he grows over-confident. Or a sub-unit might be ordered to retreat before the enemy, leading him into a trap.

Local Mobility offers many opportunities for effecting surprise, and the same principle should be applied to the siting and erection of prepared defences. Those which are to be used in earnest should be placed where the enemy can discover them (if at all) only at the last possible moment when he is already under fire. They should be skilfully camouflaged. The others, serving as dummies to draw fire, should not be left unconcealed in their pristine nakedness, but camouflaged with deliberate lack of skill, so that the enemy is deceived into thinking he has discovered a point of weakness.

4. *The commander should hold back his reserve as a striking force until the moment arrives when he can use them decisively.*

In the kind of decentralised warfare which will leave Home Guard commanders with an independent command there are not likely to be many opportunities for probing soft spots in the enemy's defences and exploiting lines of least resistance. But the old maxim of withholding reserves until the main attack (whether conducted by the enemy or the Home Guard) develops, although in general it demands larger forces than a Home Guard commander is likely to possess, has a certain limited application here. Reserves should be highly mobile and given strong fire-power. Thrown in at the right moment, they may be able to prevent a breach of the defences, and to turn defence into counter-attack. They are likely to be most valuable if they come into action at a point away from the rest of the defenders, and open fire from a flank.

Immediately they have done their job the reserves should be reformed and recalled to headquarters. Essentially the small body of reserves at the disposal of a Home Guard commander should be used (*a*) for reinforcement; (*b*) to stop infiltrations; (*c*) to bring extra fire power to bear on the enemy when he shows signs of disorganisation and demoralisation.

5. *The commander should make sure his plans for defence or attack are not too rigid. They should allow his subordinate commanders a certain freedom of action and offer them alternative routes for advance and withdrawal.*

In real warfare plans can only rarely be carried out to the letter. Too much is uncertain, and the situation is always changing. The commander should keep his object (main purpose) clearly in mind, and remember that there are various ways of attaining it. His plan should therefore, within limits, be variable. If it becomes unwise to use one road, he must switch to another. If he cannot cut off the enemy's line of advance at one point, because time has been lost, he must quickly find another place for his interception. Above all, he must avoid planning an operation which may succeed entirely, but, if anything goes wrong, utterly fails. In war something always goes wrong. The eggs must not be put all in one basket. The good commander lives—as a commander—from hour to hour, holding inflexibly to his object (main purpose), but always ready to use one of several means of attaining it. Whatever does not further his object is useless and should be rejected. The commander cannot be everywhere at once: he should therefore be sure that his subordinate commanders understand his object, and, subject to that, they should in attack or defence have alternative courses open to them, of which they must choose the one most likely to yield success.

6. *The commander should not renew an attack in the same place or by the same method once it has failed.*

This principle embodies one of the bitterest and most costly lessons of the 1914–18 war. Even if the enemy defence has been shaken (knowledge not always available to the attackers), an identical repetition of an attack only makes things easier for him. If the attack is renewed in the same place, another method, or other weapons, must be used. Very often the best resource is to rely on Local Mobility, to withdraw quickly and come in again from another quarter. But, generally speaking, once an engagement has begun the commander can rarely influence it except by the employment of his reserves.

Field Exercises planned and conducted on these lines ought to yield valuable experience. Some can profitably be undertaken first by day and later by night. Their general effect is similar to that of drill in the handling of weapons. By repeated practice commanders and men learn to apply principles in action—a much more difficult task than the definitions and analyses here undertaken—and doing the right thing at the right time becomes more or less instinctive. A man in battle undergoes certain violent impressions on his nerves and his senses. These impressions are apt to distract him from his duty and confuse his thinking unless he not only knows, but can unhesitatingly carry out, the basic actions required of him. He needs to be thoroughly rehearsed before the first performance. It is the purpose of field exercises to supply the necessary rehearsals.

CHAPTER V

TEN SPECIMEN FIELD EXERCISES

Field Exercises No. 1.

CLEARING A SMALL WOOD OF ENEMY ON FOOT

(See Diagram 4)

ON no account should the wood be entered from all sides; otherwise men are almost certain to fire on their own comrades, and amid the confusion and recriminations some of the enemy may escape. The most satisfactory method is to make a drive through the wood with a line of moppers-up. A V formation, covering the whole spread of the wood, is sometimes prescribed, but experiment has shown it to be impracticable, for the Home Guard at least. Alignment is difficult to maintain, and where there is thick undergrowth even the general direction may be lost. A single line for a straight drive through seems a better proposition. The commander should take post with a small mobile reserve and, on either side of him (but also behind

TEN SPECIMEN FIELD EXERCISES 89

Diagram 4
Clearing a small wood of Enemy on foot.

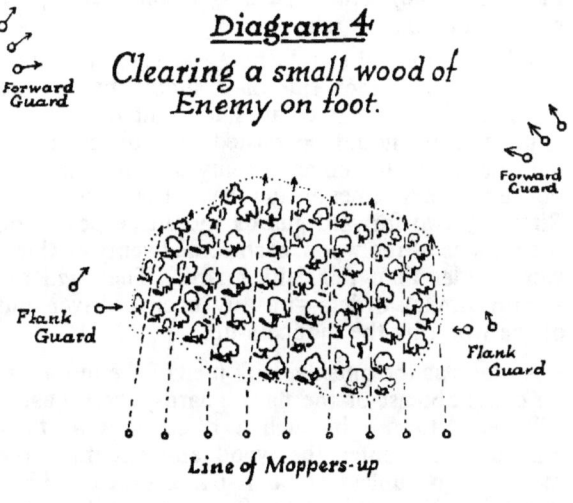

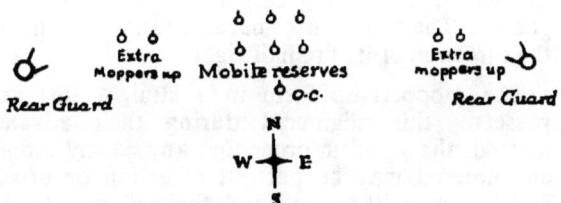

the main line), small parties of moppers-up to carry out a final search.

While the wood should not, and usually cannot, be surrounded, each side of it should be covered by fire. To prevent escapes to right or left two flank guards should be posted, one on each side with orders to fire on any enemy who emerge—but not until they emerge and have been identified. Similarly two forward guards should be posted on the far side of the wood, each some twenty or thirty yards wider than the flank guard. They will fire —with similar orders—on any enemy driven out of the wood by the moppers-up.

As soon as the outside flank men of the moppers-up come abreast of the flank guards, these guards will cease to fire in such a direction that their bullets would enter the wood and endanger the moppers-up—unless at point-blank range. When this point is reached the left flank guard will change direction half left, i.e. across the further end of the wood, but taking care to avoid the forward guard. The right flank guard will similarly change the direction of its fire half right.

The moppers-up form in a straight line and preserve this alignment during their advance through the wood in order that any enemy groups encountered may be put out of action or driven out to where the flank and forward guards can fire on them.

TEN SPECIMEN FIELD EXERCISES 91

Behind this line of moppers-up proceed the mobile reserves—with whom the operational commander might well place himself. Their task is to move swiftly towards any centre of determined resistance and put an end to it. On either side of the reserves should be placed small parties of extra moppers-up.

Two small rear-guards are left behind, one on each flank, to deal with any enemy who escape the sweep of the moppers-up and mobile reserves.

The moppers-up should proceed cautiously and quietly, disclosing themselves as little as possible and taking cover. They should search any pits, thickets, ditches and other suitable places in which the enemy may hide. From time to time they will halt to preserve formation. Inside the wood the enemy has a distinct advantage. He will have chosen firing positions in cover, and may well be able to inflict casualties before he is forced to retreat or surrender. To minimise these casualties the moppers-up should show themselves as little as possible, and move swiftly from one point of concealment to the next. They should be warned beforehand that each man is to halt, as he reaches the farther margin of the wood, so as not to cross the field of fire of the flank and forward guards.

The most suitable arms for this operation are rifles with fixed bayonets and tommy guns (sub-machine guns). The mobile reserve should carry in addition light machine guns and hand grenades. The grenades should be used only under the commanders' orders, to dig out the enemy from a pit or watercourse: and it should be borne in mind that fragments of grenade casing may carry as far as a hundred yards.

The task of clearing a wood should not be undertaken except in daylight or very strong moonlight. During hours of darkness, posts should be established round the wood, roughly in the positions indicated for forward, flank and rear-guards, with order to fire only at short range and at identified enemies. The clearing operation should commence as soon as the light is suitable.

Field Exercise No. 2

DEFENCE OF A VULNERABLE POINT BY OUTPOSTS

(See Diagram 5)

FOR this exercise platoon may be opposed to platoon, or two sections against another two. If the scale of the forces used is increased the operation becomes more complex, and it may be as well to mount the attack from two widely separated points of the compass, even N.—S. or E.—W.

In this example the defence commander's dispositions are governed by the situation of the vulnerable point to be protected, the local topography, and the expected direction and strength of the enemy advance.

The enemy is assumed to be a body of parachutists proceeding on foot to sabotage, and perhaps to keep a rendezvous or seize transport on Laburnum Road where the vulnerable point is sited. The defence commander—his right flank and rear secured by other Home Guard forces—realises that he has not enough men to push forward into the wood with any reasonable hope of engaging the enemy decisively there. As the ground slopes down from the wood towards the west and is open there, he depends on his two road blocks to hold up any attempt by the enemy to proceed down these roads. (If only two sections are opposed to two, these road blocks can be assumed to be held by the rest of the platoon).

Given these data, the defence commander may dispose of his men in many ways, and the one indicated on the diagram is put forward only as a basis for discussion. In any event, variations must be made to fit local topography. But the principles on which the diagram dispositions have been made are worth considering.

Three outposts are put out as near to the direction of the enemy's advance as is safe. Outpost A is highly mobile, with cycles or preferably cars at hand. It conceals itself behind the hedge and roadsides at the bend in Raspberry Lane, and from this position can open fire on the enemy as he advances down Raspberry Lane or Blitz Road, or across the open low country to the north and west; this should give early warning of his approach to the other outposts, H.Q. and reserves, and the garrisons of the road blocks. Under pressure Outpost A will retire by road and either join the garrison at Road Block Y or leave its transport there and proceed on foot to reinforce

TEN SPECIMEN FIELD EXERCISES 95

the garrison of Road Block X, if a strong attack develops down Blitz Road.

Outpost B is furthest forward at the opening of the exercise. It is on foot, and takes station (immediately signalling its position to Outpost A) inside the wood, on the western edge. Here it conceals itself and is ready to fire on the enemy moving through the wood, down Raspberry Lane, or across open country to the west. The line on which Outpost B will retire is to the transverse ditch and hedge, where it can hope to make a stand, and then down the N.—S. ditch and hedge, breaking away to hold the weapon pit behind the vulnerable point, as indicated in the diagram.

Outpost C, also on foot, takes up its position just inside the wood near the eastern edge of the territory allotted to the enemy advance. Under pressure, or in conformity with the movements of other outposts, it will retire due south, by hedge and ditch, and make its first stand somewhere in rear (as well as to the right flank) of the first standing point for Outpost B. This is in order to safeguard itself from an outflanking movement by the enemy on its right, made under cover of the wood. Finally, Outpost C holds the other weapon pit in rear of the vulnerable point.

The defence commander establishes his H.Q. behind the vulnerable point, with his mobile reserves on the road, and a few others, not mobile, in the two forward weapon pits to cover the point. Thus Outposts B and C can retire, if necessary, wide of and covered by the two forward weapon pits, and their withdrawal during its later stages can be covered by fire from the reserves in these weapon pits.

Such dispositions ensure that the defence makes the earliest safe contact with the enemy that is possible and guard against any sweeping movement to outflank on the east by road or over open country; while if the outposts are forced back they have prearranged lines of retreat which bring two of them back concentrically on the rear weapon pits, while the third can enfilade the enemy (from Road Block Y) if he should attempt a close assault. The reserves should be withheld for meeting this assault and should only be thrown into the attack if the outposts succeed in disorganising the enemy at first or second contact. Even so, the defence commander should put in only a minority of his reserves, for fear the enemy's withdrawal is a feint.

The outposts, until they reach the weapon pits in rear, must not allow the enemy to engage them at close quarters. Their aim should be to inflict casualties by surprise and by opening fire at a useful range (200—400 yards). They must retire in due order, each outpost providing covering fire for the other, if the ground permits; otherwise

TEN SPECIMEN FIELD EXERCISES 97

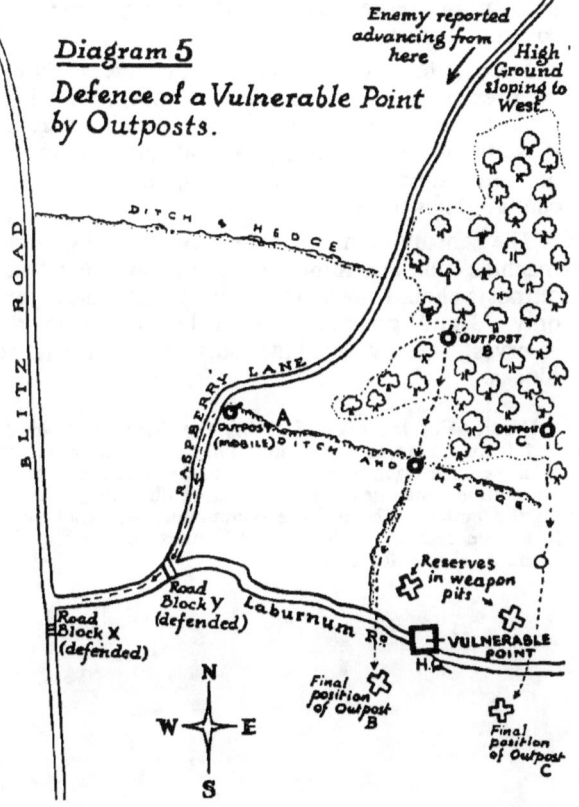

each must retire in alternate moves, one half covering the other.

In order to ensure probability of contact it should be prearranged that the enemy splits into three groups: for them the exercise will provide practice in stalking, taking cover, tactical flanking moves or infiltration, and developing fire-power on changing positions.

The enemy can be armed with rifles, light machine-guns and tommy guns. The three defence outposts should carry rifles and light machine-guns only. Hand grenades should be kept with the reserves. Heavy machine-guns go to the road blocks.

[*Note.*—For the sake of clarity the diagram is simplified from an actual map, and only one line of retreat is shown for each outpost. If local conditions permit alternative routes leading to the same ultimate positions, all the better. The defence commander will then leave it to the section leaders which routes to choose if a withdrawal is enforced.]

Field Exercise No. 3.

ATTACK ON A FARM

(See Diagram 6)

A HOME GUARD unit, in preparing its plans to repel invaders, will not normally expect to undertake the defence of a farm, unless it is used as a Home Guard headquarters. The great danger is that farm buildings are easily set on fire. If an enemy body, not in overwhelming force, is making in the direction of the farm (perhaps at dusk and after being roughly handled by other British troops) it may well be tempted to seize the farm and hold it as a fortified position; in such circumstances it would probably pay the Home Guard to let the enemy take possession and then make them sorry they ever allowed such an idea to enter their heads.

The diagram approximates closely to an actual farm, and field exercises have shown that there is no substantial increase of fire power to be effected by putting outposts into the surrounding fields, while the men holding them invariably are unable to retire on the main position without suffering casualties. The enemy, being strangers, may not realise this, and the first stage of any attack therefore should be to reconnoitre and then to overpower or cut off any outposts he may have established.

At zero hour the commander of the attacking force should be informed of where the enemy was last seen, and when and in what direction he was moving. He should also be given an estimate (which may later prove erroneous) of the enemy's arms and equipment. His first task is to discover if the enemy is in occupation and to deal with any outposts.

The wall round the farmyard is a hindrance to the defence; it may enable the attackers to come in close under its protection. The north-south stretch of the wall can be covered from the main building (Post A) but to bring fire to bear on anyone approaching the east-west stretch, the enemy (defence) commander must establish a post at the northern end of the stables and sheds. If he puts it at the north-east corner (Post F) it can also fire down Haywagon Lane. Post E, at the south-east corner of the stables, commands the main gate and to some extent Turnpike Road. Posts E and F should therefore be regarded as constituting an independent garrison under a subordinate commander. It is not likely they will be able to rejoin the main body of the defence if the attack gets to close quarters, and if any satisfactory strong point in the farmyard can be impro-

TEN SPECIMEN FIELD EXERCISES 101

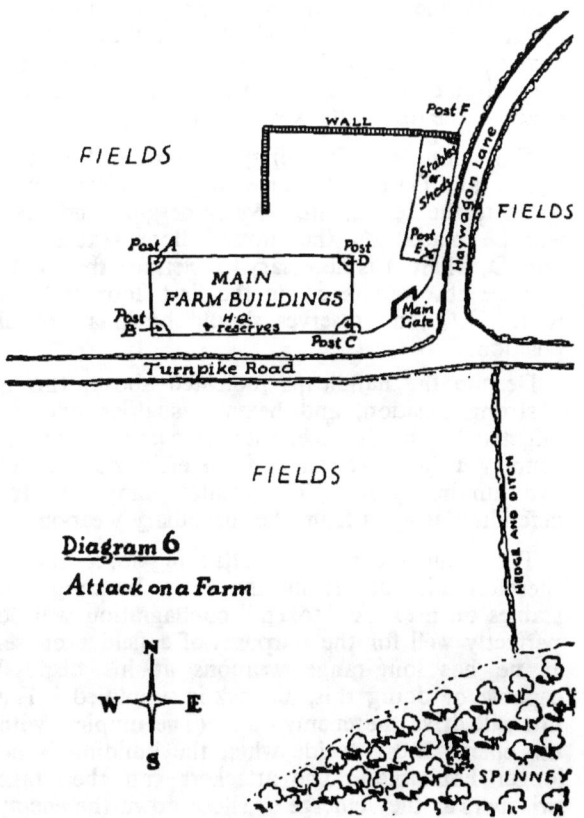

Diagram 6
Attack on a Farm

vised for them to fall back upon, so much the better. On the other hand, if the attackers force a way past them to close in on the main building, they should seize their opportunity to counter-attack in the rear or flank with short-range weapons.

The main farm building is defended by posts A, B, C and D each at a corner to give the maximum width to the field of fire. Machine guns and rifles will be placed on the ground floor (except on Post D, where it is necessary to overlook the wall); grenade throwers, etc., on the first floor and the roof. H.Q. and reserves should be in a central position.

Despite the handicaps indicated above, this is a strong position, and heavy casualties may be inflicted by the defence, with its command of the country around, at ranges from eight hundred to two hundred yards. The greatest danger to the defending army is from the incendiary weapons.

The commander of the attacking force should therefore aim at setting the main building and stables on fire. A "token" conflagration will do perfectly well for the purposes of a field exercise. If he has long-range weapons at his disposal capable of doing this, his task is simplified. The fire will drive the enemy out. (The umpires with the enemy must decide when the building is no longer habitable.) The attackers can then take prisoners as they emerge or shoot down the enemy if he tries to fight his way out. For this purpose posts must be established all round to close in as the fire spreads.

If the attack commander possesses only short-range weapons capable of setting the buildings on fire, he must find some means of getting a small party of his men to close quarters. The diagram shows that the farm commands most of the surrounding country, and there are only two feasible approaches for the incendiary party. They may come (preferably in motor transport) down Haywagon Lane and turn at speed along Turnpike Road, or reverse this approach. This must be done swiftly and the inflammable agents hurled as they go past: a hazardous and uncertain operation.

The other alternative is for the incendiary party to creep and crawl down the hedged ditch from the south or under cover of the roadside hedges. When they get to close quarters they should be covered for their final dash by fire from as many machine guns as can be brought up, either mobile on the road or firing from the spinney. To time and direct such machine-gun fire, however, is not easy. Practice and co-ordination by signal system is needed.

This exercise should be tried first in daylight, and if the attack proves too difficult, it should be tried again by night, and a note made that in real warfare any enemy in possession should be contained there until nightfall.

Unless the local strength is exceptionally high, not more than two sections should be allotted to the defence. The attacking strength should be at least equal, except by night. Both defence and attack should be equipped with heavy and light machine-guns, tommy guns, rifles and bayonets, hand grenades and incendiary weapons.

The exercise can profitably be repeated several times, attack and defence interchanging, and the attack varying its route and methods, until every reasonable probability has been well tested.

Field Exercise No. 4

HOLDING A FORTIFIED STREET AGAINST ENEMY WITH TRANSPORT

(See Diagram 7)

THIS exercise is especially suitable for urban areas, but may easily be adapted for a village. If possible, a street lined continuously with houses, neither detached nor semi-detached, should be chosen as the site for action. It is virtually impossible to pin an enemy and effect a victory in a street where gaps between houses afford ways of escape, unless the defence possesses sufficient materials, men and weapons to fortify and cover all these gaps.

In the diagram it will be seen that Main Street (where the defence commander intends to bring the enemy to action) includes a side turning to the east at the northern end, a vacant building lot on the eastern side, and a passage on the western side. These must be adequately stopped, with a road block, anti-tank obstacles and barbed wire respectively, and garrisoned.

The enemy is reported to be approaching from the north in vehicles, probably three tanks, with motor-cyclists in front, and lorry-borne infantry behind or in front of the last tank. The defence commander has already noted the large building on the south side of Market Street as a probable objective which the enemy may try to seize and hold as part of the process of infiltrating into the town or village and capturing it piecemeal. (See *Street Fighting*, p. 47.) Having prepared defences and fortified houses beforehand, and reckoning the forces and weapons at his disposal adequate to the task of giving battle to this comparatively small enemy body, he resolves to fight before the enemy reaches his probable objective at all.

The means he adopts is a variation of the tank trap in a defile; he has to reckon also with the motor-cyclist outriders and the accompanying infantry in lorries.

In choosing a Headquarters for the action and posts of his reserves he may elect to place them nearer the junction of Main Street with Market Street. The position shown in the diagram gives him a less than perfect view, but on the other hand it provides a line of communication via houses and gardens on the east side of Main Street, which should be relatively free from fire: along this line he can send and receive messages and despatch reinforcements from his reserves. He guards his rear with two weapon pits and a rear flank guard is posted in a house on the south side of Market Street, also covering road block X.

TEN SPECIMEN FIELD EXERCISES 107

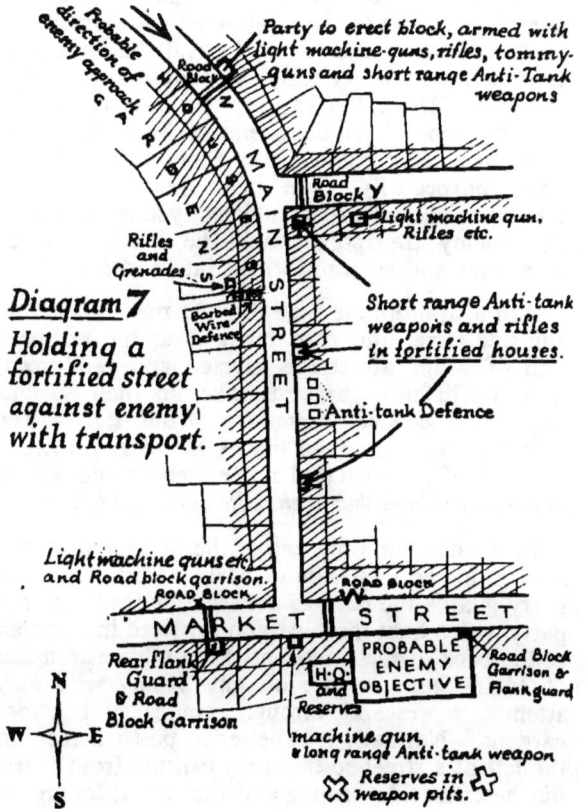

The erection of the road blocks W and X is completed, and they are reinforced with lorries and any heavy material that may be available as soon as the report of the enemy's probable approach is received. These blocks are sited just round the corner from the southern end of Main Street, so that the enemy column sees them very suddenly and unexpectedly. The main point is that a stretch of enclosed road sufficiently long to contain the enemy transport should be blocked in all directions and so transformed into a defile.

At the appropriate time the rear road block Y in the side street and road block Z at the northern end of Main Street are erected and reinforced, and the defence garrisons take up their various posts and conceal themselves from sight. The materials for these road blocks Y and Z are left at the side of the road and made inconspicuous *until the enemy column has been halted or slowed down.*

In the diagram only two of the defence posts are shown on the west side of Main Street. A small party guards the passage between houses ; another party with a light machine-gun is placed in a garden at the back of the houses at the south-western end of Main Street to fire on any enemy who may attempt to escape through houses and across gardens. Normally it is better to post riflemen on the left of a street so that they can fire from cover, but here the side turning and the vacant lot are on

TEN SPECIMEN FIELD EXERCISES 109

the right, so most of the posts are grouped there. A heavy machine gun post is established in a fortified house on Market Street, from which it can command the length of Main Street to just beyond the bend. This should be able to put infantry dislodged from tanks or lorries, and also motor-cyclists, out of action. Close range anti-tank weapons may also be used from houses here against the forward enemy vehicles.

The advantage of placing all the other defence posts on the east side of Main Street is that they are less likely to inflict casualties on each other. The men should be warned, however, not to venture into the street, down which the heavy machine gun will be firing. If the enemy suffers severe casualties and becomes disorganised, the men in these defence posts may, at a later stage, come into the street to finish the action, but only after ordering the machine gun to cease firing by prearranged signal.

The general plan of the action, then, as the defence commander designs it, is that the garrisons remain concealed and do not open fire until the head of the enemy column, probably motor-cyclists, pulls up in front of blocks W and X. The concealed garrisons of the most northerly posts then quickly erect road blocks Y and Z, covered by fire from other men on these posts. Even if the chances of battle do not allow them to erect these rear blocks, they should be able to prevent the enemy withdrawing. The enemy is thus halted and, unable to turn and escape, must give battle.

The aim of the defence should be to fall on him instantaneously from a number of positions, using machine-guns, light or heavy, tommy guns, rifles, flame throwers and other anti-tank weapons. Generally speaking, anti-tank and other grenades, Molotoffs and such will be thrown from upper windows at tanks and lorries, and S.A. will be fired from ground floor windows. If anti-tank mines or explosives are used, the detonating party must be given clear space to work in.

A company is the most suitable unit to carry out this defence, or three platoons with the other platoon taking the part of the mechanised enemy, whose arms may be augmented for this occasion.

The umpires may judge that a certain number of the enemy would escape this first simultaneous assault and take up positions in the houses on the west side of Main Street. The exercise may then enter on a second stage of house-to-house fighting. This will be useful practice, but the results are difficult to judge. If possible, one umpire should be stationed at each road block and street defence post, and at least three should be with the enemy, to estimate the effect of the attack.

Field Exercise No. 5.

DEFENCE OF A BRIDGE OVER A RIVER OR CANAL

(See Diagram 8)

THE strength of the garrison will depend on the importance of the road and the bridge carrying it across water. The road-blocks at each end will be of concrete or some other permanent material. Better results will be obtained if strong points are *not* embodied in them or sited just beside or in rear of them. This is because the garrison will probably find its view along the road obstructed, and the obviousness of the defence position may lead to the enemy concentrating high-explosives on it with disastrous effect.

In the diagram only one approach, with the appropriate defence system, is indicated, but it should not be assumed that because the enemy approaches from the north he will not also appear from the south. Even if he has crossed the river at another point, it will still be of the utmost value to deny him the use of the bridge—and relief may come speedily.

For this exercise the defence commander should not be informed of the enemy's strength or location, but left to obtain information from his outposts, which should be in visual communication with the bridge defence H.Q. and have a pre-arranged and simple system of signals.

Informed in this way of the enemy approach, the commander will man his posts, send off a message to the appropriate quarter that he expects an attack, and complete his road-blocks.

We assume that the enemy attack comes from the north. It will be met with S.A. fire from the weapon pits (each with an alternative position connected by a crawl trench) A, B. C and D. These are designed to cover the full arc of 180 degrees in which the enemy can approach the bridge and its block. He can be fired at both on the road and on the flanks if he attempts to develop an attack there.

Four bombing pits, E. F. G. and H are dug close to the roadside, and from these enemy vehicles halted or slowing up can be attacked with close-range anti-tank weapons. In addition to this, from the point X near the river bank and on a flank, long-range anti-tank weapons can be used on the enemy vehicles, and a machine-gun or other anti-personnel weapon used against the dislodged tank crews or follow-up infantry. The siting of the barbed-wire entanglement presents a problem. It

TEN SPECIMEN FIELD EXERCISES 113

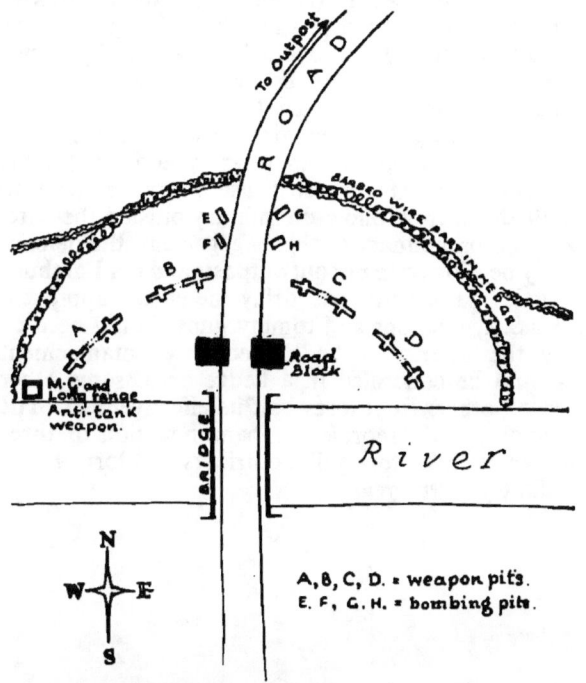

Diagram 8
Defence of a Bridge over River or Canal

must be between thirty and a hundred yards in front of the weapon pits and bombing pits, which otherwise would be exposed to attack by hand-grenades. It must not be put across the road for fear the enemy is halted too soon. This means (*a*) the road gap in the wire must be covered with heavy fire to prevent an infantry attack; (*b*) the defence commander must use every resource to halt the enemy follow-up infantry outside the wire.

As a preliminary to this engagement, the defence may be allowed to put out outposts and road-ambush parties, to obstruct and delay the enemy approach. All S.A. weapons and tommy guns should be used by the defence. The barbed wire entanglement should be concealed in a hedge or in some other way: otherwise it loses half its effectiveness. The enemy should represent a panzer section of three tanks, with motor-cyclist outriders and lorry-borne infantry in the rear.

Field Exercise No. 6

DEFENCE OF A FACTORY

(See Diagram 9)

[*Note.*—In certain areas a factory Home Guard may be required to participate in the general defence scheme. It may then have to defend its premises by taking station a mile or more away. In general, factories will continue to work even in the event of invasion, and the Home Guard duties will be principally observation and anti-sabotage. If and when the enemy draws near, the factory Home Guard will cease production and function as part of the local defence scheme. Nevertheless, defence schemes are subject to alteration, and such exercises as this should not be overlooked.]

IT is doubly important to hold a factory or works against the enemy; first to deny him occupation for either use or sabotage, and second to prevent him using the building as a temporary fortification and shelter to further his occupation of the whole town by infiltration.

The factory shown in the diagram has a fairly typical lay-out in that it faces a busy street and built-up area, is surrounded by its own fenced-in yards, and backs on to fields. The defence of factories which are closely hemmed in by other buildings involves the fortification and garrisoning of some of these buildings, patrols in vehicles or on foot, and, from the first, close-quarter fighting with such short range weapons as the tommy gun, the hand grenade and the rifle and bayonet. It can only to a limited extent be planned in advance, and training should proceed along the lines indicated in *Street Fighting*. (See pp. 47–49.)

In order to hold successfully a factory such as that shown in the diagram the defence commander must first realise that he is liable to be attacked from any side or from all sides at once: this includes air attack. So far as possible, then, he must site his posts to give each a field of fire on two or three sides.

He will doubtless consider the establishment of outposts in the fields outside the factory premises, but it is unlikely that he would be able to dig communication trenches across the factory yard to afford the outposts a fair chance of retiring under pressure. If he can do this, all the better. Otherwise he must make up his mind to resist enemy attacks from all sides mainly by fire from posts in the factory building, power-house and sheds.

The wooden fence running round the yard presents a problem; it affords an approaching enemy cover from observation and enables him to get to comparatively close quarters. On the other hand, it would yield little protection against fire

TEN SPECIMEN FIELD EXERCISES 117

Diagram 9
Defence of a Factory

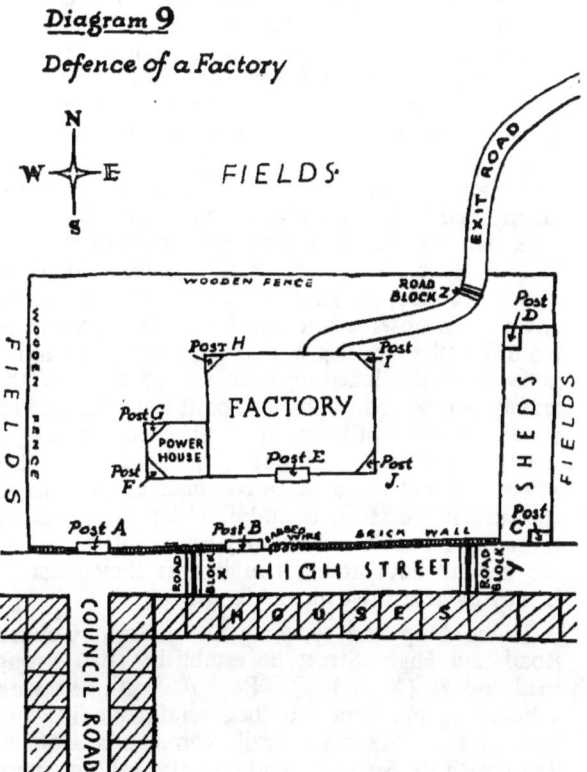

to any posts he might establish there. The defence commander has two alternatives. He can make loopholes in the fence (which we assume to be at least six feet high), and erect sandbag-walls behind them in suitable places. From these posts (not shown in the diagram) he can cover the fields to the north and west, and give the garrisons orders to withdraw to the factory and power-house if the enemy gets within a certain range. The disadvantages are that he must deplete his central garrison to man these posts, and, once they are abandoned under pressure, he yields to the enemy not merely cover from observation (the fence), but protection from fire (the sandbag walls). His other alternative is to level the fence as soon as approach of the enemy is reported. This means at least that he can sweep two sides of his position with heavy and light machine-gun fire. It has also the considerable advantage that the defence commander can station the men in Posts G, H and I, and part at least of the men in Post F, where they ought to be, i.e., on the ground floor and not higher, as they must be if they have to fire over the fence.

To hold up and repel an attack from Council Road and High Street he establishes two strong road blocks (X and Y). Post A, equipped with a bombing platform, sandbag reinforcements and loopholes in the brick wall, commands Council Road with its S.A. fire, and can also lob anti-tank bombs, and possibly grenades, on the enemy held

TEN SPECIMEN FIELD EXERCISES 119

up by road block X. Post B is the second garrison for this road block; it should be equipped also with tommy guns in case the enemy forces the block or outflanks it through the houses on the south side of High Street. If the defence commander can spare the men, he might also reinforce one of these houses and garrison it.

The main gate is commanded from Post E, and subject to flank attack also from Post B. A block, or at least a substantial barbed-wire entanglement should be erected at the gate. The most likely site for H.Q., with the reserves, is on a floor above Post E. It should afford the defence commander good all-round observation and easy means of communication within the building.

The approach from the east along High Street is guarded by road block Y, with Post C (in or on the sheds) to cover it. This is a two-sided post, and so is Post D, at the north-west end of the sheds, which covers Road Block Z and the fields to the north and east, as well as Exit Road. The men for posts C and D should be carefully chosen; they must not leave their stations if the attack develops away from them, to the north-west or the south-west; while if they are themselves heavily attacked they are unlikely to be able to fall back on the main building.

The factory and the important power house are guarded by five posts (F. G. H. I and J), each commanding two sides, as well as by Post E facing the main gate. The siting, arrangements and use of these posts should follow the principles indicated in *Street Fighting* (p. 49), i.e. riflemen and machine gunners on the ground floor and/or first floor, observers under or on the roof, and the supplies in the cellars. The walls alone should not be relied on to give protection from fire; muzzles should not project from loopholes; and rooms should be darkened.

For the adequate defence of a factory of any size, at least two platoons are necessary. The enemy should be of approximately the same strength or even more. The exercise will be more valuable if the enemy is given transport and, after the initial stage of the attack, splits into two or more parties, attacking from several sides simultaneously.

Field Exercise No. 7

A SMALL ENEMY PARTY IN A CHALK PIT IS ATTACKED WITH MACHINE GUNS AND HAND GRENADES

(See Diagram 10)

THIS exercise is suitable for two or three sections. One represents a small body of the enemy which has been driven by exhaustion, or after suffering casualties elsewhere, to go to ground in a chalk (or sand) pit or some similar place of shelter. The other two sections (or half sections) represent the attacking Home Guard, ordered out after the enemy's position has been observed and reported.

The chief difficulty confronting the attacking commander is how to " get at " the enemy, who has cover for himself from fire, yet can command all approaches to the pit. The solution is to make the enemy keep their heads low long enough for the grenade throwers to get within range.

Both attacking sections proceed by road, using cars for speed, and the rising bank for cover, to a point between the tall tree and the cottage (see foot of diagram). Here the machine-gun party leaves the cars, and sets up its gun, training it on the chalk pit. It does not yet open fire unless the enemy attempts to leave the chalk pit.

The bombing party with their grenades do not stop here (unless to confirm details of their co-operation) but proceed in cars by the circuitous road route (assumed to be off the diagram) until they reach the eastern edge of the spinney, out of sight of the enemy.

The bombing party proceeds cautiously and quietly through the wood, with flank, forward and rear guards. For the purpose of the exercise the enemy, although exhausted, need not be assumed to be quiescent. He should put out outposts in the spinney and perhaps in the ditch. It will be the task of the approaching grenade party then to overcome these sentries, if possible by stalking and in silence, before proceeding further.

At the edge of the wood the grenade throwers (not more than four) crawl along the ditch or watercourse till they come to the nearest point to the chalk pit which will still not bring them into the line of fire from the machine-gun party. The remainder of the bomber party split into a covering rear guard holding the ditch (but within the spinney) behind the grenade throwers, and another covering party, which takes post on the southern edge of the spinney and prepares to open fire on the southern edge of the chalk pit. It is this second covering party which receives the pre-arranged signal from

TEN SPECIMEN FIELD EXERCISES 123

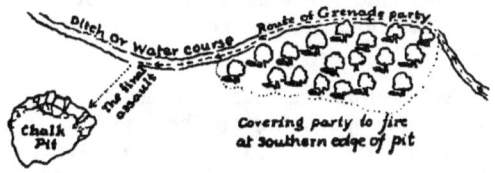

Diagram 10

Small enemy party in Chalk Pit is attacked with machine-gun and hand-grenades.

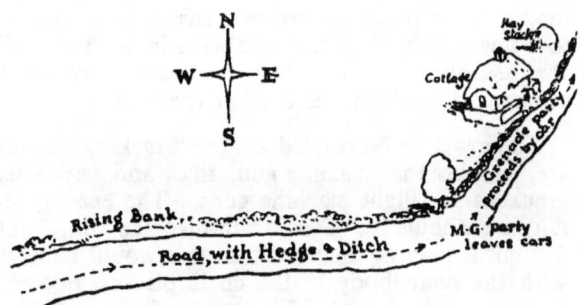

the grenade throwers that they are in position, and transmits it across country to the machine-gun party.

As soon as this signal is received the machine-gun party opens fire on the chalk pit (but taking care to avoid the ditch on the eastern flank). At the same time, from closer range, the covering party on the edge of the wood opens fire with rifle and light machine gun, also on the chalk pit. This should startle the enemy, confuse him and make him keep his head down. The firing persists only for a pre-arranged length of time—twenty seconds should be ample. As soon as it stops, the grenade throwers dash out of their ditch and at twenty yards range hurl their grenades into the chalk pit, immediately flinging themselves flat on the ground and getting their rifles into position. The moment the pieces of grenade casing have ceased to come down, they rise and dash in to finish off the assault. In this they are joined by their covering party from the edge of the wood.

The arms to be carried by the attacking parties are, besides the machine gun, rifles and bayonets, grenades and light machine guns. The enemy, in fairness, should be given a sub-machine gun, but I think it may be assumed that this would be kept with the main body in the chalk pit and not entrusted to an outpost. The most suitable time for this exercise is dusk, when such an enemy party would be most likely to seek cover for a few hours' rest. Co-operation and co-ordination between the machine-gun team and the grenade party is not easy to perfect. The exercise should also test the visual signalling system in use.

NOTE.—If a small building takes the place of the chalk pit, two machine-gun posts may be necessary to provide sufficient covering fire. Mortars and smoke bombs should also be considered.

Field Exercise No. 8

ATTACK ON AIR-BORNE TROOPS

(See Diagram 11)

A LARGE and fairly flat field (Fairmeadow in the diagram) is chosen by the enemy, who set out to seize it and use it as an airfield for fighter planes. Their method is to drop parachutists in three adjoining fields (King, Queen and Knave Fields), and five minutes later three troop-carrying planes are crash-landed in Fairmeadow itself. The parachutists gather their arms together and proceed to establish defence posts round Fairmeadow to the north and east, i.e. to cut off and hold Fairmeadow. The enemy disembarking from the troop carriers drag these planes to the edge of Fairmeadow, while some of them hasten to set up defence posts at the south-east corner and to sabotage the railway.

In view of the fact that Nazi parachutists may use uniform difficult to distinguish from our own, enemy troops for this exercise should not carry a distinguishing mark, and the troop-carrying planes can be represented by farm wagons or cars.

At zero hour the Home Guard commander receives a message from his observation post, by

TEN SPECIMEN FIELD EXERCISES 127

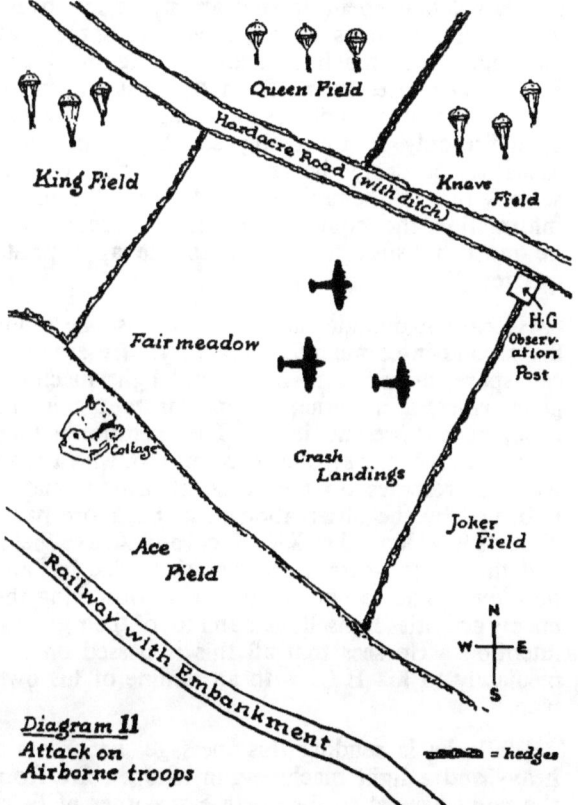

Diagram 11
Attack on Airborne troops

telephone, that enemy planes are flying low overhead. Five minutes later a cyclist from the post tells him that parachutists are landing in Queen Field. The three men left on the post will make it their first duty to observe and report; they will open fire only if by doing so they can inflict casualties or delay the enemy's activities without serious risk to themselves. That is all the initial information the commander should receive, and he must transmit it at once to the appropriate quarters.

He cannot denude his other posts, so he sends his second-in-command, with all the reserves he can spare, armed with heavy and light machine-guns, rifles, and perhaps a mortar to tackle the problem as it presents itself. The operation is then in the hands of the second-in-command, who arrives with his reserves on the scene of action, and is informed by the observation post that more parachutists have landed in King Field and Knave Field, and three troop-carriers have crash-landed in Fairmeadow. The second-in-command, observing the enemy activities himself, gets an idea of their general intention. He sees that all this is passed on immediately to his H.Q. with an outline of his own plan.

While he is sending this message, he orders a heavy and a light machine-gun to open fire from the point nearest to the north-east corner of Fairmeadow, on the troop-carriers and their late occupants, and also on the parachutists in Knave Field. With those in King Field and Queen Field he cannot deal there and then. He also puts out riflemen as flank and rear-guards. Despite all this, he may well be driven east along Hardacre Road.

He then perceives that the south-east of Fairmeadow is guarded by an enemy post. He decides whether he can send a patrol to stalk this post along the hedges or whether it will be quicker and more effective to send them round by road and find a place where they can come up from the east along the railway embankment. Whatever he decides to do, he includes in a message to his H.Q., and also suggests that reinforcements may be able to approach most satisfactorily by railway, but warns them to beware of sabotage on the line.

A little later the second-in-command may have been driven back some distance from Fairmeadow, but he will know that he is inflicting casualties and spreading the enemy's defences. After a time he should be sent a message that reinforcements from the Regular Army are coming through by road, and that an increase of fire from the railway will mean that either the Railway Home Guard unit or rail-borne troops are coming into action here. If sufficient numbers are not available to give substance to this change in the situation, the umpire should effect it by informing the enemy commander.

The second-in-command and his detached section (sent by hedge or road towards the railway) should then be able to advance again.

The defence commander's object is to observe and report, then to delay and harass: only when adequate reinforcements come up can he enlarge this to an attack. And his attacks (in co-operation with the reinforcements) should be planned to mop up the enemy dispositions, not all at once, but part by part. The principles of this operation are: (*a*) the Home Guard must not bite off more than it can chew or try to operate on too wide a front: it should be prepared to retire, inflicting casualties, until reinforcements arrive; (*b*) it should work from one or two sides only of an enemy landing; a surrounding operation is only likely to weaken its effort; (*c*) when reinforced, it should attack the enemy, necessarily dispersed, one part after another. In the exercise based on this diagram, for example, the concluding stages of the operation would be the mopping-up of the posts established by the troop-carrier enemy, and then of the parachutists landed in Queen Field and King Field, who should be left till then to guard flanks which will not be attacked in the first stages. Some of these may take refuge for a last stand in the cottage at the south-west corner of Fairmeadow.

Two sections can be set against two sections for this exercise, but if others are available later to reinforce the defence, the enemy strength can be increased to a platoon or more. Some anti-tank weapons may be carried in case the troop-carriers claim to have landed light tanks. The parachutists should be armed with tommy guns and grenades, and unless they take over quickly they may be put out of action by the Home Guard, operating from a greater range than tommy guns will carry, before they can get their heavier guns into action. The umpires should take careful note of the times at which the initial stages of the operation begin, and in subsequent practice every effort should be made to open fire at the earliest possible moment. For this, not only quick and accurate reporting is needed, but immediate decisions by the commander on the spot.

[*Note*.—For this exercise it is assumed that regular troops, probably with armoured fighting vehicles, are at hand. Home Guard commanders in country districts where such reinforcements are not immediately available would do well to form a Company Reserve, motorised, as a striking force against parachutists. If they obtain authority to armour-plate one or two cars (see page 58) these may fight from the road-side or on occasion enter fields to crush machine-gun posts established by parachutists.]

Field Exercise No. **9**

THE ENEMY MASKS THE MAIN DEFENCES AND BY-PASSES TO THE WEST

(See Diagram 12)

The Home Guard here has for its principal task the defence of a village or the outskirts of a town. The main thoroughfare is Cathedral Road, on which Church Street converges. Observation Posts A and B are established to the north on these roads. The main defences are sited further south, at Archdeacon Cross-roads, because Chantry Street affords another entry to Cathedral Road. These main defences consist of road blocks W., X and Y, to the rear of which is H.Q. with the reserves. The approach from the west, along Abbey Road and Vicarage Way, is protected by Road Block Z. Further south is assumed to be guarded by another unit.

The defence commander has been given the object of holding up the enemy attack from the north towards Archdeacon Cross Roads, and also to delay and harass any attempt to traverse his area apart from this. His main defences are round

TEN SPECIMEN FIELD EXERCISES 133

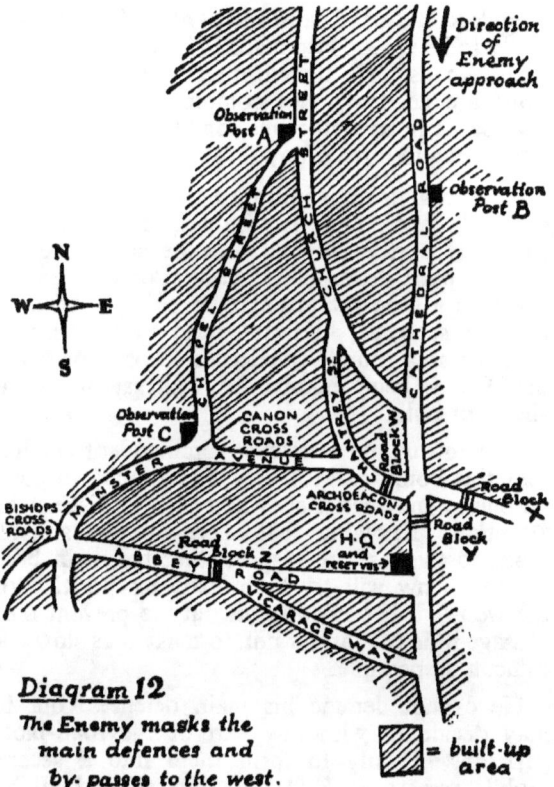

Diagram 12
The Enemy masks the main defences and by-passes to the west.

▨ = built-up area

Archdeacon Cross Roads, and he has lighter obstacles ready to be moved into place at Canon and Bishops Cross Roads. He therefore feels that his dispositions are adequate and comprehensive: he can give battle in advantageous conditions to an enemy attempting to force a way through.

At zero hour he is informed by the umpires that a strong enemy force is approaching him by road from the north. In due time he should receive more reports from Observation Posts A and B. Then, at a time pre-arranged to coincide with the enemy's schedule, he is informed by the umpires that the area round Archdeacon Cross Roads and his H.Q. is being bombarded with gas or smoke-shells, or both.

It is now up to the defence commander to deduce that this bombardment may be designed to cover an enemy movement elsewhere and to distract his attention. Knowing that there are no suitable roads to the east, he suspects that the main body of the enemy will try to by-pass his position on the west. It is obviously his duty to prevent their passage if he can, and if not, to make it as slow and difficult as possible.

He cannot denude his main defences, but he may decide to withdraw part of the road-block garrisons, if only to form them into a second mobile reserve at H.Q. He himself and all his men must now be wearing respirators. The only route which will take the enemy clear past his flank is Chapel Street, Minster Avenue to Bishops Cross Roads and so on southwards. He must therefore rush his reserves, under his second-in-command (with or without the addition of men withdrawn from road-block garrisons), along Abbey Road to Bishops Cross Roads. There they can remove their respirators. If the enemy is not in sight they should make their way to the observation post at Canon Cross Roads. At one or other of these places the second-in-command must improvise dispositions and erect the light obstacles which will enable his men to give battle, if possible with a surprise effect, but without unduly exposing themselves to counter-fire. The houses on the west side of Minster Avenue should be used as firing points, and the fight should be maintained southward from the opposite side with short-range anti-tank weapons. If obstacles can be erected in the roadway, all the better, but the materials should be those which are at hand there normally, or wire, etc., carried with the mobile reserves.

If the umpires adjudge the enemy to have been turned back at Bishops or Canon Cross Roads, the enemy should retire at speed along Chapel Street and quickly make another attack in force down Church Street or Cathedral Road. It will then be up to the second-in-command to leave a small garrison on the scene of the first engagement, and take his reserves back to H.Q., where the defence commander will need them for holding road-blocks W, Y and Z.

The exercise is intended to test the application of the principle of Local Mobility, the alertness and adaptability of commanders, and the qualities of the men under their command in the face of a changing situation and unexpected disclosures of the enemy's intention.

Field Exercise No. 10

THE PINCERS MOVEMENT AND COUNTERSTROKE

(See Diagram 13)

THIS exercise is suitable for both town and country units, and is well worth practising because, although the expression " pincers movement " belongs properly to strategy, Germans meeting a Home Guard centre of resistance are quite likely to employ a double, converging attack with the object of enclosing the defences by a part of their forces—which will be left behind for this purpose, while the remainder moves on by a by-road. It is most important that Home Guard units should anticipate this, and discover in practice the method of defeating the enemy's intention most suitable to their own particular terrain.

If the enemy appears in such force that he can afford to unloose a detachment to deal with the resistance, the local Home Guard can do only one useful thing about his main force: observe closely and report quickly and accurately. The next thing for the unit commander to decide is whether he can afford to give battle from his defences against the enemy detachment with a fair prospect of destroying them or at least of repulsing them. Moreover, he must make this decision in good time to allow him (if he is in danger of being overwhelmed) to withdraw his men and carry on the fight elsewhere. Orders from higher authority may lift from him the responsibility of making the decision: it may very well be his duty to stand his ground and fight it out against whatever force the enemy can bring against him. But if he is exercising an independent command, he must obtain all the early, accurate information about the enemy he can, because whether he decides to stand and fight or to make a withdrawal and take up for the time being a guerilla rôle, his decision must be swiftly but not lightly made. For this exercise the defence commander is assumed to have such an independent command and full responsibility for the movements of his men.

There will be only a minority of Home Guard positions which are not liable to a converging attack. In the diagram the road system may be either in a built-up area or in open country. The enemy, in unknown force, but moving by mechanical transport, has been heard of in the north proceeding southward. The defence commander's rear is adequately covered by other dispositions, omitted from the diagram to simplify it.

Realising that the enemy may approach by way

TEN SPECIMEN FIELD EXERCISES 139

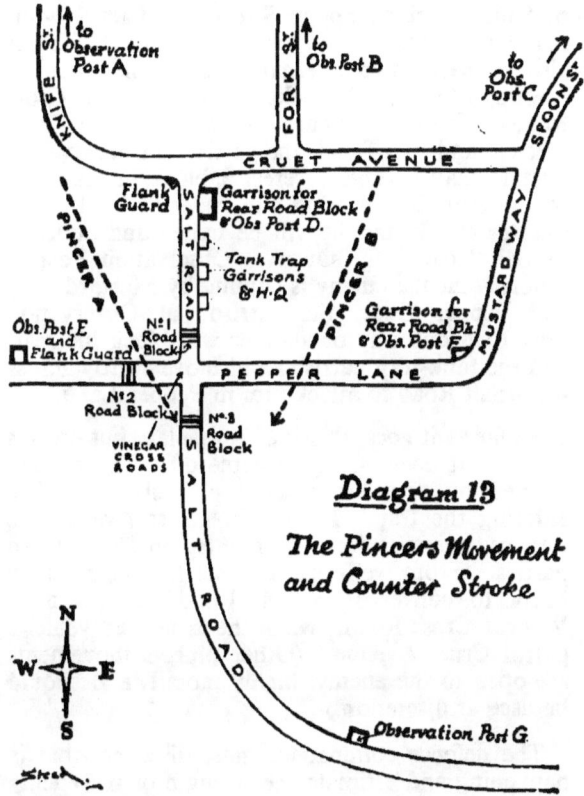

Diagram 19

The Pincers Movement and Counter Stroke

of Knife, Fork or Spoon Street, the defence commander has put out outposts A, B and C. He has also prepared two alternative anti-tank traps by erecting three road-blocks at the Vinegar Cross Roads. If the enemy approaches by way of Cruet Avenue and Salt Road, the garrison at observation post D may be able to erect a block in his rear; in any event it will bring him under fire and close-quarter attack, and he will be halted and attacked in Salt Road. If, however, Observation Post C reports that the enemy is coming by Mustard Way and Pepper Lane, the garrison at Observation Post F in one way or another will block his rear, and the tank-trap garrison will move swiftly across from Salt Road to attack him in Pepper Lane.

So far as it goes, this is a likely plan, but on this occasion it does not quite come off. The enemy, warned by previous experience, pulls up before entering the trap. Halting in Cruet Avenue, he puts out a strong force of infantry on foot, in two parties. From well-separated starting points they begin to converge on Salt Road just south of Vinegar Cross Roads, while the armoured vehicles patrol Cruet Avenue. (Other pincers movements are open to the enemy, highly mobile, and should be used at discretion.)

The defence commander must discover what is happening and estimate the strength of the enemy in relation to his own. Then he must decide either to stand and fight round and about Salt Road between Cruet Avenue and Pepper Lane or to get out while there is time to keep his men together and in fighting trim. For organising such a withdrawal the defence commander should use every means of speedy transport and maintain flank guards and rear-guard. (Long before the operation begins he should have selected and made known two alternative rallying points outside his inner defences.) He should make a "token" destruction of valuable stores and papers, and use smoke-bombs (to cover his retreat) and grenades, tommy guns and the rifle and bayonet for any close quarter fighting that may be forced on him. But his principal aim should be immediate decision, speed, a high morale in his men, and as few risks as possible until he is ready to renew the fight. It will depend on local topography whether or not he needs a simple system of signal communications to make the order to withdraw immediately effective.

If he is alert and lucky, he should be able, using his local knowledge, to hold the enemy with his rearguard near Vinegar Cross Roads, while concentrating the rest of his force to surprise one or other of the enemy pincers from a flank, and put them out of action. His aim should then be to let the enemy converge on defences no longer held, to outflank the outflanker, and surprise the enemy just as he begins to suspect that his own surprise has failed.

Just to make things more difficult, the umpires should see that the defence commander receives —at a hard-pressed moment—from two of his outer observation posts reports of the movement of the main enemy body which has sent a detachment to attack him. These reports he must pass on *at once* to the appropriate quarters.

For this exercise the Home Guard unit which will in action be responsible for the defences should act as a whole, and the enemy should be drawn, in equal strength at least, from another Home Guard unit or from regular troops.

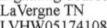

www.ingramcontent.com/pod-product-compliance
Lightning Source LLC
LaVergne TN
LVHW051741080426
835511LV00018B/3170